# Golden Years

## of

# Sheffield

*The publishers would like to thank the following companies for their
support in the production of this book*

## Main Sponsor

## The Wolf Safety Lamp Company Limited

AMB Limited

H Askey Transport

Associated Chemists (Wicker) Limited

Atkinsons of Sheffield

Edwyn Blyde Limited

H Harrold & Sons Limited

Record Tools Limited

Enos Kaye Limited

BWD Rensburg

T W Sampson & Company Limited

Sheffield Sports Stadium Limited

Stainless Plating Limited

Swann-Morton Limited

H Turner & Son Limited

W K West Limited

Wolstenholme Machine Knives Limited

First published in Great Britain by True North Books Limited
England
HX5 9AE

ISBN 1 903204 13 5

*Text, design and origination by True North Books Limited
Printed and bound by The Amadeus Press Limited*

# Golden Years

## of

# Sheffield

# *Contents*

# Introduction

I t is only when we pause for a moment and look back that we realise just how much our lives, and the city we live in, have changed over the decades. Some changes came about so naturally and gradually that we barely noticed them. Others, initiated by outside forces, were sudden and shocking. During the blitz of the second world war, many familiar city centre landmarks disappeared literally overnight - Atkinsons, Walsh's, the Brightside and Carbrook Co-op among them. Reconstruction was a slow process, and many readers will remember the city of their youth littered with derelict buildings and bomb sites. Many, too, will remember the demise of the old tram network, when people turned out in droves to see Sheffield's last tram. Sociologists theorised over the new phenomenon of the tower block at great length while the residents of the new blocks found out for themselves the pros and cons of high-rise living. Demolition of cherished buildings including the Nelson Hotel and the King's Head caused some controversy, and new creations such as Tudor Square and Arundel Gate gave Sheffield an unfamiliar, altogether more modern aspect. Alongside these changes, our own habits were altering. We discovered supermarket shopping, and barely noticed the old corner shops disappearing.

Fargate, complete with floral traffic island, in a scene from 1957

We watched television and were not affected by the closure of one more cinema. More and more families had cars. Post-war generations quickly took for granted items which to the previous generation had seemed fantastic, extravagant luxuries, as technology revolutionised our leisure and our working lives as well. And society adjusted its values. Women, for instance, asserted their right to equality in the workplace - and here Sheffield certainly did not lag behind: in June 1965 Sheffield Stock Exchange welcomed its first woman member and became the first stock exchange in Britain to allow a woman onto its trading floor.

In this book we have included photographs of Sheffield before, during and after the second world war. We look back on the days when little girls wore white ankle socks, little boys wore shorts, and there were no denim jeans to be seen; when entertainment, as often as not, meant a visit to one of Sheffield's 69 cinemas to see a full programme including a B-movie, newsreel and a feature film, all for as little as eightpence - though the best seats in the house would cost you two and fourpence; and when Sunday tea was likely to be a pork pie from Davy's. We hope that these pictures will bring back happy memories for older readers, while those too young to remember may be able to gain a clearer impression of what life was like for their parents, grandparents and even great grandparents.

# *Around the city centre*

Few photographs could evoke the atmosphere and bustle of Sheffield as we once knew it. The barrows and piled up boxes outside the Sheaf Market (more commonly known as the Rag and Tag); the knots of shoppers dodging between the passing cars; people standing on their doorsteps watching the world go by; the old lorries, cars and trams; the adverts on the hoardings that were once so familiar. And spot the old one-horsepower vehicles on the left of the photograph, which remind us of the gentler age when the city's only traffic pollution could be shovelled up and used on your floribunda!

The advertisements alone give us a taste of real nostalgia: Bass, Rowntrees Cocoa, Ewbank carpet sweepers, Bisto, Wills Gold Flake, Players, Bovril, and others which we cannot read. Remember the simple slogan, 'Ahh Bisto!'? Few realise that the name Bisto is itself a hidden slogan, being a rearrangement of the initial letters of 'Browns, Seasons, Thickens In One'. Neat - and composed around 1910. We got used, too, to the slogan 'Great stuff this Bass'. Remember the character Bill Stickers who was shown in the Bass adverts, sticking the slogan across an Egyptian pyramid and in other unlikely places?

**Bottom:** According to the film critics, the cast of 'Men of Tomorrow' was more interesting than the film, which they labelled as 'a dim comedy'. Emlyn Williams, Merle Oberon, Robert Donat, Maurice Braddell and Joan Gardner featured in this British film, which centred around the goings on between a group of Oxford students. Released in 1932, the film was already three years old when it came to Cinema House in Fargate. Though not nearly as large as some of the city's cinemas, Cinema House was nevertheless as richly decorated as some of the larger establishments. It was equipped with comfortable sofas and dark blue upholstered seating, tapestries of hunting scenes, a refresh-ment room, and an open balcony above the street where patrons could take tea in the summer time. Cinema House opened in 1913 - the era of silent films, of course - and while many cinemas relied on the services of a pianist, who adapted the music to suit the drama or romance of the film, Cinema House boasted a 12-piece orchestra to provide the accompaniment. Eventually, as with so many of Sheffield's familiar land-marks, Cinema House fell victim to the red pen of the planners and was demol-ished in the early 1960s for redevelopment.

**Right:** Readers who were motorists back in the 1940s and 50s will remember with a sigh of regret those days before yellow lines and the volume of traffic banned us from parking outside the city centre shops. The familiar 'waiting limited to 20 minutes in any hour' signs were the thin edge of the wedge; we could leave the car near the shops, but we had to be fast on our feet! How many incurred parking fines, we wonder? This Union Street photograph is dated 4th May 1950, and in the background a few people have decided to 'get away from it all' for a while and are setting out for a day in the country or by the sea - though number of the hats and warm coats worn by the day trippers indicates that the weather was not the bucket and spade variety. On the opposite side of the street, a day trip is out of the question for those who have to put on their overalls and go to work. Two of the workers are making heavy weather of erecting a sign above a shop window - and it is to be hoped that the plank they are standing on is more sturdy than it looks!

Comparison with older photographs taken in this same spot in High Street makes us appreciate that in a place where jay walkers at one time abounded, the pedestrians using this crossing on 19th April 1952 were behaving in a very orderly manner! It was the appalling accident statistics which led to the creation of the very first pedestrian crossings, and these were to become a remarkably effective road safety device. Marked out by studs and yellow beacons, the crossings were introduced in 1934, and with a fine disregard for the behaviour common to little boys, the first beacons were made of glass. So many of the glass globes were broken that the design was quickly changed and they were replaced by globes of painted aluminium. The date given for our photograph raises more questions than it answers, as across the country, pedestrian crossings were given their white stripes in 1951, and the beacons became plastic and began to wink in 1952. That being the case, this one was a little behind the times, but it would not have been long before High Street had its fully-equipped zebra crossings.

Rush hour traffic and a heavy downpour are not the ideal mix of circumstances, and people running to get out of the rain seem to be taking their lives in their hands. Though there are a number of private cars in this shot of the Haymarket, public transport was for the vast majority of people the only way to get home after work. For this was 1946 - a year after peace was declared - and a family car was an undreamed of luxury for people who were simply glad that they had survived the war intact. The city took a real battering during the blitz, and properties on the left of the photograph fell victim to the Luftwaffe's bombing raids. Spot one of the wooden temporary shops which were hastily built to provide premises for some of the bombed-out businesses. The bombing raids affected the trams as well as buildings, with six employees killed and fourteen other staff members injured while they were on duty. Fourteen tram cars were hit in the raids and turned into heaps of twisted metal. Much of the track and overhead wires were also destroyed, bringing the tram service to a halt until emergency repairs could be made.

Victoria's disapproval. She denied him any access to state papers, and he was ill-prepared for his role as King. Prince Edward was 59 when he at last became King Edward VII, and in the event his reign was a short one of nine years - he died on 6th May 1910.

**Top:** What has caught the attention of the two schoolboys in the foreground, we wonder? The lovely old saloon car, perhaps - or maybe they are collectors of car registration numbers, as many little boys were at the time. Well into the 1950s the old pre-war cars were in the majority on Sheffield's roads, but those who could afford to buy new vehicles were finding by the middle of the decade that car designs were beginning to change. Mudguards and running boards like

**Above:** Queues have formed inside the tram stops in Fitzalan Square back in 1950. Appropriately, the square today is the hub of the new tramway system - a direct echo of the old days, the Supertram having brought us full circle. The Burtons building, in the left background, was badly damaged in the blitz, and stood derelict for many years. The stony gaze of King Edward VII - eldest son of Queen Victoria and Prince Albert - surveys the scars of war which still remain in Fitzalan Square in 1950. The Prince's story is a rather sad one, and is worth relating to readers who like to know these things! Known to his family as Bertie, the Prince had waited a long time to become King (and if his royal mother could have done anything about it, he never would have been!). His lack of academic ability, coupled with his fondness for pretty women, good wine, cards and expensive clothes earned him Queen

those on the 'sit up and beg' design of the old pre-war cars were set to become a thing of the past; headlights would be faired-in and incorporated into sleeker body lines, flashing indicators would replace the semaphore type (remember how easy it was to forget them and leave them sticking out?), and even quarter-light windows would gradually disappear from our cars. This nostalgic view of London Road captures two delivery vans outside Davy's. Which of our older readers cannot remember Davy's legendary cornish pasties and pork pies? And their tomato sausages? Marvellous with a rasher of bacon and a couple of fried eggs! Adjoining Davy's was W E James & Co, where the keen gardener could buy anything from a bag of tulip bulbs to a draw hoe. Quick Press Ltd were not a printing firm - a notice in their window offers to press the flannels of passers by.

**Above:** Traffic holdups are not a 21st century phenomenon, as this memorable old photograph reveals! This line of slow moving traffic in London Road (impeded somewhat by Davy's delivery van, which was being unloaded at the time) was recorded on 5th October 1949.

The number of small shops in the shot is interesting; remember the time when small grocers like Gallons were a common sight around Sheffield? Sadly, many of them are gone, together with the personal service we once took for granted. Small grocery chains and corner butchers were the traditional way to shop, and customers would queue to be served while the grocer weighed out our butter and sliced our bacon on his machine on the counter. A far cry from today's plastic packs! People might have had to wait a while longer to be served, but at least they had the benefit of personal attention from the staff. Things were to remain that way until the mid-1950s, when self-service shopping began to catch on.

**Below:** Apart from public transport there was little traffic around in Moorhead when this view was recorded in 1939, and the prominently displayed notice on a tram standard which warns motorists that the standing limit for unoccupied motor cars is 20 minutes would appears to be quite unnecessary. Motoring was, in those days, a middle class privilege anyway, and few among the working classes would have aspired to owning their own car. The days when almost every family would have at least one vehicle lay far in the future! Behind the oncoming tram lay the Nelson Hotel - an establishment which, thirty years or so on, was to have a tragic murder committed on the premises. The Nelson was completely rebuilt in 1963, when its interesting architecture was swept away to make way for a building which was typical of the 'square block' designs which were favoured among the architects of the day. The aforementioned crime took place in the late 1960s, and the pub was at the time still the Nelson. It was later renamed The Hind, and still more recently it went through yet another name change, becoming Seamus O'Donnells.

**Below:** Among the things money can't buy is what it used to! Meals and accommodation at the four-star Grand Hotel, whose tall facade we can pick out to the left as we look along Leopold Street, is a case in point. Though we have no figures available for the time of the photograph, a few years on a bed for the night and a full English breakfast at the 180-bedroom hotel would have set you back at least £3.10s.

Wilson Peck in the left foreground was *the* music store in Sheffield, and more than a few of our readers will have rocked around the clock to the records they bought there! Our photograph was taken in the late 1950s, when rock 'n' roll was the new music favoured by the young. The parents of the aforementioned young who were true music lovers might also have visited the store and splashed out on a good radiogram or even a piano. Wilson Peck would not

only sell you the piano but would, if you wished, arrange music lessons for you, while their tuners would make sure that your valuable instrument was kept in good order. Interestingly, the building was originally the premises of Johnson & Appleyard, and the plaque reading 'Cabinet makers to the Duke of Norfolk' is still on the wall.

**Bottom:** Window shopping with a difference was offered at Atkinsons back in September 1950. The air raids of December 1940 turned much of The Moor into a wasteland of rubble, twisted metal and smoke-blackened walls leaning at crazy angles. Atkinson's department store was totally destroyed that night; the next morning revealed a scene of devastation - the roof, walls, windows, floors and all the stock had completely gone. The site was eventually cleared and levelled, but five years after the war had ended

vast areas of Sheffield still needed to be rebuilt. Atkinson's had reconstructed display windows but the rebuilding of the store still lay in the future. One of Sheffield's few family firms, Atkinson's new store was eventually reconstructed on its original site. Advertisements are as much part of our nostalgic glimpse through time as the buildings they appeared on, and readers will remember the familiar ad for Good Year tyres. Back in the 1950s few motorists concerned themselves too much over the amount of tread on their tyres. A decade on, however, this aspect of road safety had become a matter of public concern. When Barbara Castle brought in the first tyre law in the mid 1960s, specifying the minimum legal depth of tread which a tyre must have, tyre sales rocketed.

**Above:** This marvellous view of Castlefolds fruit and vegetable market dates back to the 1930s. As we can see, there are a number of lorries and cars around but the preference with a number of these traders was obviously the good old horse and cart. The old fashioned method of transport had fewer breakdowns, emitted no pollution apart from the useful used fodder in place of petrol and returned your affection! We might assume that these traders were unloading goods to sell in the market, but they were just as likely to have been loading up with stock to take out on to the roads and sell around the residential areas. An old three wheeled truck takes up much of

the foreground; affectionately known as the mechanical horse, these wagons were indeed a useful workhorse. This one belonged to the LMS. The covered part of Castlefolds Market can be seen in the left background; a memorable view, this, as the market was closed in the late 1950s and became part of Parkway Wholesale Market. The Norfolk Market Hall, built in 1851 at a cost of around £40,000, dominates the right background.

**Above right:** 'No Waiting' warn the signs which sprouted across the city during the 1960s to keep motorists off the streets, and on the day this view was captured in March 1965, not a single driver was around to challenge

authority. The Moor - seen here from Young Street - was in fact quite car-free, and the young mother with her baby, and the few shoppers who were about, need have no fear of crossing the road. Milletts' three display windows are crammed with goods; wouldn't it be fascinating to be able to see the prices and compare them with today's? Back in the 1960s, denim jeans had already become entrenched as the fashion of the decade - though they were in fact to remain popular right up to the end of the 1990s. Levi Strauss began to manufacture jeans in the 19th century, mostly for gold miners, and interestingly, they added the now-familiar rivets as reinforcements to stop the weight of the gold nuggets tearing the pockets.

**Below:** Isn't it amazing how familiarity can breed, if not contempt, at least inattention? Hurrying to get out of the rain, the few passers-by in Union Street are occupied by affairs other than the Victorian splendour of the Newton Chambers Showrooms, and would rarely if ever stop to admire the ornate building with its showy domes and flamboyant architecture. Love it or hate its lavish style, the building was in fact part of the city's history; it was constructed in 1893, and as readers will perhaps already know, its claim to fame was that it was the first iron framed building to be built in Sheffield. About to become part of Sheffield's redevelopment area, Union Street wears an air of desolation and impermanence. The old showrooms were about to be developed by the Boden Group as a store and office building; Newton Chambers had a vast industrial complex at Thornecliffe, near Chapeltown. Name anything in iron, from gates and railings to gas pipes, and Bodens could come up with the goods. Our photograph was dated 1968, and future years would see many changes, not least the nearby roundabout in Furnival Gate.

**Bottom:** The 7th November 1953 signalled another shopping day in the Haymarket, and the usual buzz of pedestrians in our shot keeps the police officer busy. Some of these eager people, shopping bags in hand, would have been making for Woolworths, where the food was good and the prices affordable, both in the cafe and all around

the store. The first Woolworths stores in the UK were called '3d and 6d Stores' - a direct echo of the original Woolworths '5 and 10 cent Stores' that spread in a chain across America at the end of the 19th Century. F W Woolworth, who in 1879 opened his first stores selling a wide range of goods at fixed low prices, had a chain of over 1,000 shops in the USA by 1911. With his brother C S Woolworth he later expanded into the UK, Canada and Europe. This branch of Woolworths was eventually closed and a new building constructed not too far away, which was opened in 1961. The new Woolworths was built on the site of the old Norfolk Market Hall, and older Sheffielders still have a soft spot for the old market. Its Penny Bazaar was a huge hit with the bargain hunters of Sheffield!

**Bottom:** Though passers by are wearing coats and caps, a row of open windows in the Town Hall inform us that though this might not have been the warmest day, a little fresh air was nevertheless still needed. Sheffield's Town Hall was built rather later than those of other northern cities; Sheffield had other, more pressing demands on the public purse at the time. However, the land was obtained in 1886, and a competition for the best design was launched. Of the 178 entries the design of Mr E W Mountford was chosen, and 21st May 1897 was a red letter day for the city when Queen Victoria herself came along to declare the new Town Hall officially open. The magnificent building has lost none of its excellence with the passing of time - its 210ft tower, topped with a very appropriate seven-foot figure of Vulcan, the god of fire, is as much appreciated today as then. Each of its four clock faces measures an incredible 8ft 6in in diameter. To the left of the photograph is the Albany Temperance Hotel, beloved in time gone by among Sheffield's visitors from overseas, today it is the premises of the Yorkshire Bank.

**Right:** It was wartime when this view of the Wicker was captured for posterity. Though some damage was done at the Wicker Arches, these buildings survived the blitz. A number still stand today, among them the Grosvenor Hotel on the left of the photograph, taken on 24th August 1943. A mystery object stands outside Lewis's shop; close inspection reveals that what appears at first glance to be a large box is in fact a brick structure.

What it was and why it was built is unknown to us. A large sign outside The Grosvenor tells us that this is a Gilmours house. Duncan Gilmour's & Company was founded around 1830, at first as a wines and spirits merchant. Thirty years on, they moved into brewing and were based at Furnival Brewery in Furnival Gate. Gilmour's were an ambitious company and expanded by taking over other breweries until they themselves were eventually taken over by Joshua Tetley's. Our view takes in other interesting buildings: standing taller than the adjoining properties on the right approaching the Wicker Arches (which can just about be seen in the background) is the headquarters of Samuel Osborne & Co, steel manufacturers, today the Sheffield & District Afro-Caribbean Community Association.

**Above:** Old photographs of High Street all reveal the same fact: drivers seem to lack a sense of direction when they reach this wide junction! With no convenient lanes marked off, and large white-painted arrows to guide them, as have today's motorists, the drivers of old tended to follow their own instincts when turning left or right.

**Below centre:** Four years or so after the war, things are stirring in High Street and constructor's huts are in place on the levelled site of Walsh's department store, which had been built by John Walsh back in 1899. Sheffielders with long memories will never forget 12th December 1940 -

Driving must have been even more hazardous once darkness fell, for this was 1943 and the wartime blackout restricted drivers to showing a downward directed pinpoint of light. Obstructions were painted white so that they could be seen more easily; the lamp standard in the foreground, for example, which would shed no light on High Street until 1945, and the pillar box outside the National Provincial Bank on the left, have been treated in this way. The edges of the pavement have been marked out in white and the safety rails in front of the trams (known to most as 'dog catchers') have also been painted. The safety rails were a clever innovation which would have swept dropped parcels, dogs - and the odd human - away from the tram's wheels. The building on the left with the imposing portico was, of course, the offices of the Sheffield Telegraph and Star.

and the empty, burnt out shell of the once magnificent store, the pride of the city, after the night-long air raid. Christmas presents had to be purchased elsewhere that dreadful year.... Building restrictions meant that rebuilding work was slow to get underway, but in May 1953 Sheffield got its brand new Walsh's. But the grandeur of the old department store with its delightful restaurant and orchestra, and its good quality fashions and furnishings, is still remembered by many. Rackham's later took over Walsh's store, in turn becoming House of Frazer, then T J Hughes. The photograph, taken from the upper deck of a tram, looks towards the old Kings Head Hotel in Change Alley, also sadly lost to the city. Arundel Gate would eventually be built here.

**Above:** Fashions come and go, but it is doubtful whether teenagers will ever again wear the white ankle socks and sensible shoes worn by the young girl in our photograph! Yet as recently as the 1950s, girls of up to 15 wore socks without batting an eyelid. It was an accepted part of life - especially when it came to school uniform - and nobody stopped to question it. It was not until they were around 15 or 16 years of age that girls would be allowed to wear stockings, at least at the weekend. Our photograph shows that even in 1953 Sheffield still bore the scars of war, and one of the temporary, single storey shops which were hastily built to help out shopkeepers who had been bombed out, can be seen on the left of the picture. To the right, above the trams, we can see the Norfolk Market Hall.

The market hall was built by the Duke of Norfolk on the site of the old Tontine Inn. Readers will remember the cast iron fountain inside the market hall; in 1949, to celebrate 50 years of municipal ownership, the fountain was painted in cream, green and gilt and given a pleasant rockery.

**Above right:** A service as rare as hen's teeth in our city today - a parking attendant who directs the motorist to an empty space! This particular car park made temporary use of the site of the old Corn Exchange - destined to become the Park Square roundabout. Built by the Duke of Norfolk in 1881, fire destroyed the Corn Exchange in 1947. The building stood, however, for 17 years until it was eventually demolished and the land levelled not long before this scene was recorded in 1964, in readiness for the city's ambitious road building scheme. The solid building in the left background was at one time W H Smith's wholesale premises, later becoming the headquarters of South Yorkshire Passenger Transport Executive, which it remains at the time of writing. The premises of the Canal Wharf and Warehouses can be seen in the right background, while on the far horizon, tower blocks stand out against the sky. Sheffield had suffered badly during the second world war, when 1,000 homes were destroyed in bombing raids, and the city suffered from a severe housing shortage. New council housing offered a partial solution, but in the architects' book the only way was up, and up went the new tower blocks, some of them 17 storeys high.

**Right:** These fine buildings in Leopold Street mercifully escaped the red pen of the planning department and still survive today. Firth College, on the right - named for the Sheffield industrialist and one-time Mayor Mark Firth - was Hallam University's forerunner. The College was opened back in 1879 by Prince Leopold, the eighth child of Queen Victoria and Albert, the Prince Consort. Part of Orchard Street, where the College stood, was renamed Leopold Street in the Prince's honour. The old Central Grammar School next to Firth College was probably still open at the time of the photograph - 1952. A Number 60 bus bound for Fulwood waits at the bus shelters outside the College to pick up passengers. These shelters were a useful size, occupying the full depth of the pavement as well as a decent length, providing the bus company's customers with reasonably effective protection from the vagaries of the British weather. A point worth noting is that the shelters appear to be roofed with glass panels, all of which seem to be in one piece. Though the 1950s were far from being vandal free, vandalism was not a national pastime with the under 20s. How many hours would such a set of glass panels last today?

**Below:** During the second world war, slogans rained down on the British public like confetti on a June bride, and one of the most often quoted was 'Make do and mend'. New materials and supplies of every kind were like gold dust, so whether you were making a dress or building a wall you had to make do with what you had carefully hoarded or the few materials which were available. The construction industry was hard hit, and when your home or business was damaged in the bombing raids you faced a long wait for repairs of any kind. Thus it was that as late as 1950 - the date of our photograph - Gerrards, the well known furriers on the right of our High Street photograph, had to operate from the ground floor of their building, having lost the upper floors in the blitz ten years earlier. This was of course a number of years before the tide of public opinion swung violently against the wearing of fur; fur was still very much a fashion statement in the 1950s, though thankfully few collars were seen still bearing the head of the unfortunate animal! But faux was the way to go, and 20 years on lay the heyday of 'fun fur'.

**Right:** The displays in Cole Brothers' windows are generating an enormous amount of interest - dozens of people appear to have gathered outside. Add that to the long row of motor cars which stand along the kerbside and we can imagine that a sale is in progress. Cole's sales were always an event with shoppers who had an eye for a bargain, and buying a dress or coat for a few shillings less than the normal selling price was well worth queuing for. Cole's corner was busy on any ordinary shopping day, often with people who had arranged to meet friends there. Coles' interior was quite different from other department stores, having a series of connected rooms rather than a large hall. Later years would see Coles move to Barker's Pool, opposite the City Hall. Across Fargate readers will recognise the Independent Building as well as many familiar shops such as T C Palmers, Etams and Atkinson's Fargate store. Standing proudly against the skyline is the 210ft tower of the Town Hall. Opened on 21st May 1897 by Queen Victoria, the building's exterior walls were constructed with Stoke Stone from Grindleford, Derbyshire. The architecture of the Town Hall is heavy with symbolism; Two 36ft-long sculpted friezes depict aspects of Sheffield's industry, while representations of Electricity and Steam decorate the main entrance arch. Awesome, as today's youngsters would say.

**Below:** A steady stream of traffic rounds the bend from Attercliffe Road into Staniforth Road, and the usual knot of pedestrians risk life and limb as they dodge between lorries and trams. No wonder there was national concern about accident statistics! In the late 1940s, the approximate time of this photograph, our roads certainly had pedestrian crossings - rafts of them - but they were only marked out by road studs and were not given their zebra stripes until 1951. Our eagle eyed readers will perhaps be able to identify the premises of Wigfall & Son Ltd in the background of this Attercliffe shot. The sign above the window tells us that this was their furniture department, but in actual fact you could buy or rent just about anything from Wigfalls, including their inexpensive cycles, (made, according to the local humorists, from surplus gas piping!). Wigfalls - affectionately known, you will remember, as 'Wiggies' - were one of the first stores to get into television rental back in the 1950s; you could also purchase goods on hire purchase, and countless young couples furnished their home courtesy of Wiggies and their 'never never' facilities!

**Above:** The people of Sheffield love a night out as much as anyone else, and ever since vaudeville and the music halls gave way to moving pictures, the cinema has played a key role in the city's choice of entertainment. The choice of cinemas was wide, and in the days when people went to the pictures several times a week they were all well patronised. Our nostalgic photograph will bring back memories of Barker's Pool as it was in 1952, when the Gaumont and Cinema House faced each other across the busy main road. The elegant white tower and striking dome of the Cinema House had been a well known landmark in the city since the cinema was built back in 1913, when silent films were the only option. Though experimental displays of sound equipment were mounted, Cinema House was one of the last in the city to install the new technology. Its first talking picture, 'Climbing the Golden Stair', was shown in February 1930. The Gaumont - huge in contrast with the 800-seat Cinema House - opened in 1927 as The Regent. The newer of the two cinemas converted to sound in June 1929, and charged no extra for its screening of 'Show Boat', starring Laura La Plante and Joseph Schildkraut.

**Below centre:** The busy centre of Attercliffe has long been known as a fine and busy shopping centre, and our mid 1940s photograph includes two of its larger, well known stores. On the left in Attercliffe Road is Littlewoods Department Store; the large chain store was started by Liverpool's Sir John Moores, one-time chairman of Everton FC. Born in a public house near Manchester, Sir John made his fortune from football pools and mail order. The store has not changed ownership over the years and is today Littlewoods Catalogue Clearance stores. In the top left corner of the photograph you will perhaps recognise John Banners department store - and you may already be aware of the store's claim to fame. For the benefit of those who are not, we can repeat that Banners was one of the earliest shops to install escalators for the convenience of its customers. Escalators (at that time, of course, with wooden treads) were the latest marvel of the day - and the escalator's great attraction to children seemed to have been in running up the down side!

A busy day in the Haymarket, and interestingly this busy junction demands the services of two police officers to cope with the volume of traffic and the large numbers of shoppers. The date was 22nd July 1961, and the shot includes some of the popular vehicles of the day such as the Standard 10 in the right foreground - and spot the Morris J4 van on the right. Sheffield's changeover to motor buses has been made at the time of the photograph, though the tramlines still remained. With an eye to the scrap value of the rails, some cities around Britain dug up their tramlines when motor buses replaced their trams. Not so Sheffield, which simply covered them up with a new road surface. The old rails still come to light from time to time when our ever present road works unearth them. Woolworths new store was under construction when this scene was recorded, and a long length of hoarding separates the building work from the many pedestrians. Directly opposite was Davy's, on the corner of Castle Street, and the well-known gents outfitters Weaver to Wearer in the adjoining premises - a favoured place to buy your suits, shirts and sports jackets.

**Below:** A sunny April day at Cole's corner, and pedestrians who have somewhere to go stride out to get there. The young man in the foreground looks as though he's bound for Bakewell! So busy was this crossing that two police officers were needed. Why, we wonder, did one have a white coat and the other not? Facing us is Kingdon's tobacconist's, a dying breed today. Back in 1952, the date of our photograph, however, there were many tobacconists dotted around the city, often stocking sweets and chocolate as well as cigarettes. The only advert in plain sight is one for Wills Gold Flake cigarettes, but those were the days of Senior Service, Woodbine and Craven 'A', whose unbelievable slogan during the 1920s and 30s was "For your throat's sake, smoke Craven 'A'". The first real cancer fears came in the 1960s, and from 1965 all cigarette advertising on commercial television was banned. From 1971 advertisers entered into a voluntary agreement with the Department of Health to declare the dangers connected with cigarette smoking, and 'Cigarettes can seriously damage your health' appeared at the foot of adverts. The campaign only struck home however, with slogans such as 'Cancer cures smoking'. Makes you think....

**Bottom:** Motor cycle enthusiasts will immediately spot the distinctive fish-tail exhaust pipe on what is almost certainly a Velocette LE. And what about the gear the rider is wearing? How things have changed since 1953, when motor cyclists were not obliged to wear safety helmets! Today's emphasis is far more geared towards safety, and riders are well protected by their leathers and

helmets, which come in many different colours. The Haymarket was as busy as usual, and the lady on the left is obviously finding some difficulty in discovering just how to dodge between the cars and the oncoming trams and get across the road. The date was 7th November 1953, and the day was obviously a cool one judging by the coats, caps and headscarves we can spot in the crowd. During the 1940s and 50s the very practical headscarf, that could be folded away in a pocket or handbag and brought out in wind or rain, was very popular, though many ladies preferred to wear a neat little hat. The ladies in our photograph were in good company, however - Her Majesty has long been a keen wearer of headscarves.

**Bottom:** The splendid Victorian Yorkshire Penny Bank, on the right, was built in 1888-89. The Temperance movement was in full swing by the mid 1800s, and sharing the massive building with the bank was the Albany Hotel, an alcohol free establishment, whose main entrance was in Surrey Street. With the closure of the hotel in 1958 came a number of changes: not only was the building converted to offices, but its rather nice dormer windows and chimneys were removed and replaced with a piece of modern architecture. Practically, it provided the offices with additional light, but aesthetically it did nothing for the building. Adjoining the bank is Carmel House, the premises of the YMCA, who later moved out of the city centre. Its huge Schweppes sign was a familiar sight for many years, though during the 1960s there was no need to mention the company's name - all you had to say was 'you know who...' - and you knew who! Such is the power of TV advertising! Not to be outdone, Guinness too mounted a large sign above Wallis's ladies fashions - and theirs was illuminated. In the centre background, the Sheffield Telegraph and Star's clock tower is still a landmark. The figure of Mercury, the Roman messenger of the gods, has recently been restored to the building.

**Right:** This bank on the corner of London Road and Cemetery Road, together with the surrounding properties, took a real battering during the second of Sheffield's wartime air raids. The 12th December 1940 had seen the first of the deadly raids, when all night long the crunch of falling bombs was heard around Sheffield, and hundreds of people who were in town for their pre-Christmas parties and dances found themselves racing for the shelters. Two nights later the planes were back again to deal out more death and destruction - and the bank was one of the victims. Well into the 1950s, many damaged properties still lay derelict, while empty plots of land around the city reminded us of the shops and houses that had once stood there. The bank, however, was rebuilt - though future years were to see a dramatic change in the use of the building. Today's customers are not queuing to pay in cheques or use cash machines; Roman candles, rockets and silver fountains are on offer these days at the Chinese fireworks company who now occupy the premises. The Sheffield and Ecclesall Co-op with its marvellous arcade lay across the road at the time of the photograph; today a branch of Safeways stands in its place.

**Above:** There was a time when high streets around the country were sprinkled with an assortment of different shoe shops: True-Form, Freeman, Hardy and Willis, Saxone, Dolcis, Timpson, Stead and Simpson, Barratts, Bata - there they all were. Is it imagination, or are there fewer shoe shops about today? Some of these well-known independent stores are, of course, still with us, though others perhaps have been swallowed up by the larger chains. At the time of our photograph, the prevailing fashion in ladies' footwear was stiletto heels and pointed toes. Generations of daughters have traditionally ignored their mothers' warnings in every area of life, and the girls of the 1960s were no different. They paid no heed to the words of the mothers who told them that their fashionable footwear would lead to foot problems in later life. Were they right, we wonder? Adjoining True-Form at the time was Woolworths, and a prominent sign advertises their cafeteria - a popular place for a shopper's snack on Saturday lunchtimes. Further down the Haymarket on the same side of the road, we can see that the new Woolworths is under construction - and nine months after motor buses replaced our trams, the tramlines are still on view in the Haymarket.

**Below:** Isn't Christmas marvellous? Every shop you enter glitters with tinsel, Christmas trees and gifts, but it's after dark that Sheffield comes to brilliant life with hundreds of coloured lights that sparkle like gems in the darkness. Older readers, however, might be forgiven for thinking that Christmas was more fun in their younger days. In today's commercially-minded society, Christmas trees, coloured lights and elaborate decorations find their way into the shops around the end of September, along with the endless gifts we are expected to spend hundreds of pounds on. We would not wish for a return to the poverty that marked the early years of the 20th century, when Santa left few if any gifts in children's stockings - but oh, for a return to those simple, non-materialistic Christmases! However, even the old 'hole in the road' looks special in this Yuletide view, which was caught on film in 1967 soon after it was opened. The open topped subway in High Street was officially named Castle Square, though just about everyone called it simply 'the hole in the road'. Is there any truth in the rumour, we wonder, that the subway - today the Castle Square Supertram stop - was filled in with rubble from Hyde Park flats? The area is quite unrecognisable since Arundel Gate was laid down and so many modern buildings constructed.

# On the big screen

**This page:** This photograph of Fitzalan Square in the 1950s will give readers a nostalgic trip down Memory Lane *(right)*. The News Theatre sits cosily - though differing greatly in style - between the imposing Barclays Bank building on the one side and the Bell Hotel - a Tetley's House - on the other. The site of the News Theatre had been associated with entertainment since the turn of the century, when displays of animated pictures were shown at an establishment known as Wonderland. In 1911, the Electra Palace cinema was opened, and the design of the building, its innovative facilities, and its imaginative programmes, established it as a firm favourite with cinema-goers. There was no need to miss any of the programme; not only could audiences take afternoon tea in the first floor lounge, but people could if they wished have refreshments brought to them in their seats! The Electra introduced a 'come when you please, leave when you please' policy - the first of the continuous shows which were to gain much popularity in later years. The Electra Palace closed in July 1945 and opened around six weeks later as a Capital and Provincial News Theatre. Perhaps this view was captured during the school holidays - a Disney film and the Tom and Jerry Cartoons advertised would hold particular appeal for the kiddies. In a time when television was still a novelty to the vast majority of people, the News Theatres which sprang up around the country during the 1940s quickly gained popularity. People kept in touch with what was going on in the world - particularly relevant during the war - through the newsreels which were shown continuously from three in the afternoon until 19.30 at night. Every two hours saw a change of programme. Although Britain had a television service as early as 1936 (suspended during the second world war), few people could afford to buy the expensive sets - and the range of programmes was very limited anyway. A night out at the pictures was a popular pastime during the 1930s and 40s - in fact in 1939 an incredible twenty million British people went to the cinema every week. Television became a way of life during the 1950s, and sadly the writing was on the wall for many of our popular cinemas. The News Theatre found its services redundant and in January 1962 it reopened as the Classic cinema *(top)*.

**This page:** How many of our readers remember the many pleasant hours spent at the Classic Cinema in Fitzalan Square *(right)* - possibly followed by a good Sheffield curry at the Indus Restaurant? (Remember its familiar genie logo?) The cinema started life as the Electra Palace back in 1911, and the building's elegant facade won the praise of many for its imaginative design. When talking pictures became the latest technology, the management of the Electra Palace was swift to install the necessary equipment, and on 6th January 1930 they opened the doors on their very first sound movie, 'Movietone Follies of 1929'. The cinema was the last word in luxury, with roses and greenery arranged tastefully at the front of the auditorium, plush tip-up seats, imaginative decor, cleverly placed electric lighting and stained glass windows. As the second world war ended the cinema closed for renovations and a change of use, and on 8th September 1945 it reopened as the News Theatre - which many readers will remember. By the 1960s, television had given us ready access to the news, and the News

Theatre went through yet more alterations and renovations. This time, the ornate facade which had become a familiar landmark in the city disappeared behind typical 1960s-design cladding, and the Classic Cinema was born, its huge logo informing passers-by that it was 'the best any time'.

When our view was captured on the 26th November 1982, the Classic, part of the Cannon group, had already closed its doors to audiences for the last time. The final film, 'Rocky III' had been shown two days earlier, and the building already wore an air of desolation. No photographs advertised forthcoming attractions in its glass cases, no display boards announced new programmes of films, and the cinema's glass doors stood firmly shut. Attempts were made to make this a listed building - an honour it surely deserved - but the pleas of campaigners fell on deaf ears. For two more years the Classic slowly decayed until fire swept through the old cinema on 15th February 1984, putting a final end to any thought of preservation *(below)*. The burnt-out building was later demolished.

**Above:** A row of taxis outside the Picture House in Barkers Pool are waiting for the lucky few who are enjoying a night out at the cinema - a seasonal treat, perhaps, judging by the twinkling Christmas tree near the cinema. 'High Noon' was showing at the time (our nostalgic photograph dates from around 1960) so their money would have been well spent. An American film released in 1952, 'High Noon' established itself as a classic and a firm favourite, no less so today than 50 years ago. The age-old struggle between good and evil was the theme of the western, which starred Gary Cooper as a marshal with high principles, defending his town single-handed against a bunch of desperate baddies. There was no doubting the tension and excitement of the production, and the film's message, though soft-pedalled and unobtrusive, was definitely present. The beautiful Grace Kelly - who went on to marry Prince Rainier, becoming Princess Grace of Monaco - starred opposite Cooper. Few of us will forget the princess's tragic death in a motor car accident. At the time of the photograph, the price of admission to our cinemas guaranteed you a full programme that included a 'B' movie, the latest news, a cartoon, trailers of forthcoming attractions and the 'big picture'. Those were the days!

The foyer of the Gaumont was ablaze with light, though Barkers Pool was empty of pedestrians when this view was caught on camera in the Christmas of 1960. The Town Hall clock informs us that the time is 5.35pm, so we can assume that most people are on their way home after a long day at the office. The cinema started life as The Regent back in 1927, and the opening programme included a concert as well as the screening of 'My Best Girl', which starred everyone's sweetheart, Mary Pickford. The Gaumont lost its battle for life in 1985, and it was demolished to make way for a controversial new cinema and shopping complex. Who can ever forget Prince Charles' 'carbuncle on the face of Sheffield' comment which set the cat running loose among the pigeons? Many would agree with the heir to the throne's poor opinion of the new development, while others argue in its favour, praising its imaginative design. Others still keep their own counsel and prefer to keep their thoughts to themselves. Love it or hate it however, the new complex is here to stay, at least for the foreseeable future. Who knows - perhaps some future plan to demolish it will raise a storm of protest about the destruction of our 'city's heritage'?

**Bottom:** 'An old fashioned heartwarmer' was how critics described the film 'Lassie Come Home'. Though only Roddy McDowall got a mention on the canopy above the Rex Cinema's doorways, a very young Elizabeth Taylor also appeared in the film, enchanting audiences everywhere and making her indelible mark on the cinema-going public. Readers will no doubt remember going to see the succession of 'Lassie' films, but 'Lassie Come Home' was the first and without doubt the best. The dog - which had to be sold by her poverty-stricken family - made an incredible journey to return to the people she loved; the story-line tugged at your heartstrings and was a huge success. The people of Sheffield were no exception; they loved it, and long queues wait for the doors to open in our memorable 1940s photograph. The modern design of the cinema makes it hard to believe that the Rex was built during the 1930s and opened just a few weeks before the outbreak of the second world war. The Rex, on the corner of Mansfield Road and Hollybank Road, was built to seat 1,350 - an ideal size during the heyday of the cinema, but over-large when the influence of television began to take its toll of cinema audiences. The Rex closed at the end of 1982 with 'Gregory's Girl' and Chariots of Fire'.

**Right:** This was the old Cinema House in Fargate back in 1932 - and we cannot help but be struck by the number of men - some of them obviously very young - hanging around. With presumably nothing to do and nowhere to go, we can be reasonably safe in assuming that they were out of work. The effects of national depression were still being felt - in fact as late as 1939 two million were still on the dole. A national Unemployment Fund had been created in 1928 - a pitiful sum that was barely enough to keep alive on, yet incredibly unemployment benefits had been cut by ten per cent only the year before our photograph, and the hated 'Means Test' introduced to examine the personal circumstances of those applying for aid. Every now and again it was possible, however, to scrape a few coppers together for a visit to the pictures, and 'Rookery Nook' and Conan Doyle's 'The Missing Rembrandt' were being shown at Cinema House when this revealing scene was captured for us. Only a couple of years earlier Cinema House had shown the film 'Climbing the Golden Stair'; not only was this the cinema's first talking picture, but it was also shown in colour - a great innovation at the time.

deeper and paid 1/10d to book their night at the cinema. The Wicker came through the wartime air raids - though not unscathed, and survived both flood and fire. It went through several renovations in its long life, and became Studio 7 in 1974 - but closed its doors for the last time on 20th August 1987.

**Top:** A fairly unmemorable programme was playing at the Odeon in Norfolk Street when a photographer recorded this scene for posterity; Rock Hudson was cast opposite Paula Prentiss in 'Man's Favourite sport', while 'Tammy and the Doctor' was the 'B' movie. The date of the photograph is 1964, and the stiletto heels and knee length skirts among the passers by were typical of the fashion of the day, and the Morris Minor was a popular car of the decade. The Odeon has an interesting history. The partly built post war edifice (which was actually begun in 1939 and postponed for the duration of the war) had to be demolished, redesigned and completely rebuilt owing to the city's plans for a new ring road. The original design was very ambitious, and included shops and offices as well as a 2,326-seat cinema. The new Odeon provided seating for 2,340 on two levels and its crimson velvet seats, wall to wall carpeting, comfortable sofas and the latest sound and projection technology, made the cinema luxurious enough to satisfy any cinema-goer. The new cinema opened on 16th July 1956 - and closed again in June 1971, going 'eyes down' to Bingo the very next day.

**Above:** The X-rated 'Blood is my Heritage' and 'Teenage Frankenstein' were playing at the Wicker Picture House when our photograph was taken in March 1958 - the kind of film which became common when the cinema was converted to a triple screen theatre in 1974. The Wicker was built before World War I, but in the event, only opened as a cinema in 1920, though stage shows as well as films were put on by the management. The success of moving pictures was by no means assured back then, and it was as well to have more than one horse in the race, just in case! Failure, however, was not on the agenda. People flocked to view the modern miracle, and they were prepared to pay the high price of 9d for a seat on the ground floor. The balcony seats commanded even higher prices, and Sheffield's more affluent citizens dug

**Both pages:** Thirty years separate our two views of the Gaumont Cinema in Barker's Pool, and the contrasting shots show the changes and modernisations which had been made during the intervening years. There were not as many as one might have imagined - though the 1952 view retains the cinema's original name The Regent. Built in the days before talking pictures, The Regent was opened on 26th December 1927. The cinema had a good-sized stage, a number of dressing rooms and a Wurlitzer organ as well as a screen and projection equipment, and live shows could be staged as well as films. The Regent and The Central screened Sheffield's very first talking pictures on the same evening. It is difficult for those born into this age of technology to understand exactly what an impact sound had on the cinema-going public - this was a mind-blowing step forward! The 17th June 1929 was a memorable date in the city's calendar, with 'Show Boat' being shown at The Regent and 'The Singing Fool' at The Central. Perhaps our more mature readers will remember how they shed romantic tears over Jolson's rendering of 'Danny Boy' - destined, of course, to become everyone's favourite song. The famous (and often mis-quoted) line 'You ain't heard nothing yet' was spoken by Al Jolson in the film. The 1920s and 30s were the heyday of the cinema, and the huge auditorium - lit by 5,000 concealed bulbs - was built to accommodate an audience of 2,300. The prices charged suited every pocket, with admission ranging from 8d to 2/4d. Though very simply designed on the outside, The Regent's interior was comfortable and luxurious. Gleaming mirrors and sparkling cut glass chandeliers hung in the foyer, and an imposing marble staircase led away to the first floor. The lounge, with its tasteful wall paintings and cherry red upholstered easy chairs and settees had the atmosphere of an Italian garden. You could take tea, if you so wished, in the Georgian refreshment room, which was open to the general public. The Regent was renamed the Gaumont as early as 1946, and survived the advent of the silver screen in the corner of everyone's lounge by twinning and then tripling its premises in 1969 and 1979 under the Rank organisation. It showed its last films in November 1985 before being demolished and replaced with the controversial development we know today.

# The Wolf Safety Lamp Company (Wm. Maurice) Ltd - an illuminating history

There can be few more absorbing stories than that of The Wolf Safety Lamp Company Sheffield, who have been manufacturing safety lamps for nearly a century. They survived the instability of two World Wars, various economic depressions, a direct hit from an incendiary bomb on the Saxon Road Works in 1940, but most damaging of all, the decline of the coal mining industry, their major market up to the late 1970s both at home and abroad. The Company is best known and remembered however, by the founder's daughter, Monica Maurice, a member of the Company for over sixty years, and a director for fifty. She was a woman in a unique position in the man's world of the 1930s. She became one of the most respected engineers in her field, the first elected female member of the Association of Mining Electrical Engineers, and served on many standardisation and safety committees. When she was asked how she so skilfully competed in what was traditionally a man's world, her response was simple, 'by being better'. Her son, John Jackson, now manages a business that has successfully diversified its product range for applications in the petro-chemicals, explosive atmospheres and fire-fighting safety markets. Under the family management, the Company has become a world leader and innovator in the production of safety lamps for surface industries. Her grandson, Alex, a graduate in Product Design from Brunel University continues the tradition, having joined the company seven years ago and recently being appointed Technical Director. Through his initiative the Company's research and development department was established, enabling it to adapt and develop new products more quickly, especially to meet the latest European Directives governing the safety equipment market.

The family owned business will celebrate its centenary at the end of this decade, having been originally acquired under licence by William Maurice in 1912 from Friemann & Wolf GmbH of Zwickau in Saxony. With the imposition of the 'Trading with the Enemy Amendment Act' in 1916, William Maurice was able to purchase the entire British business of The Wolf Safety Lamp Company, formerly

*Above left: William Maurice at the 'Elms', Hucknall in 1908. Above right: Wolf Safety Lamps on display in November 1937. Below: A view of the Zwickau works in 1927.*

FRIEMANN & WOLF G.M.B.H. ZWICKAU i. SA.
GRÖSSTE SPEZIALFABRIK FÜR GRUBENBELEUCHTUNG.

owned then managed by Richard Cremer of Leeds, on 1st July 1916. As a result, the business became totally independent from the German Parent Company, but a working relationship was reformed in the 1920s and continued until the outbreak of the second world War. In the post-war era Friemann & Wolf rebuilt their business again, but this time based on their West German site in Duisburg to concentrate the Company's remaining assets and expertise in one location. By the early 1980s they began to specialise solely in specialist battery technology, which they continue to do today as market leaders.

One could speculate that had it not been for Carl Wolf and his patented invention of 'the benzene' fuelled re-lightable flame safety lamp in 1882, Wolf Safety of Sheffield would not exist today. Equally, had Wolf, himself the son of a miner, not met Heinrich Friemann who assisted him with his patent application, and then financed the formation of a registered manufacturing company two years later, Friemann & Wolf would not have become the giants of lamp production, dominating the world of mine lighting across the globe for the first four decades of the twentieth century. By 1907, Friemann & Wolf were producing

numerous models of spirit, oil and acetylene safety lamps, and some of the very first electric mine lamps. The year 1915 marked the production of the one millionth Wolf Miners' Lamp, a figure that was not doubled until 1947, because of the intervention of two World Wars. By the late 1920s, Wolf in Germany had developed a refined version of the nickel cadmium accumulator safety lamp, together with a powerful compressed air driven turbine lamp designed for coal face lighting, a type of product which is still in production in Sheffield today, though substantially developed and improved.

*Left:* An early letterhead. **Top:** *The Saxon Road works in 1933.* **Below:** *William Maurice at a conference at the Royal Agricultural Hall, London in the late 1930s.*

In Germany alone, Friemann & Wolf employed over two thousand workers in seven cities and had fabrication plants in Poland, Czechoslovakia, China, Japan, USA, India and South Africa, with agents throughout the world. The exception was Great Britain, where The Wolf Safety Lamp Co.(Wm Maurice) Ltd., of Sheffield remained solely owned by the Maurice family. Monica Maurice joined the company in 1930 when, having an affinity for engineering fundamentals and also as a linguist, she embarked on the first of many visits to Germany. She was first apprenticed for a period in Zwickau in the research and development department, and then oversaw the modifications and re-labelling of Wolf lamps for the emerging British market. Indeed, a specific area of the factory was dedicated to William Maurice for production, research and development, as can clearly be seen on contemporary plans. The roles of 1912 were now reversed. The original rigid agreement was long in the past and the titans of world lamp making were happy to be producing prototype and pre production Wolf lamps, modified to William Maurice's own patented designs.

Nevertheless, had the original agreement been unacceptable, this would certainly not have deterred William Maurice from making many other significant contributions to safety in the coal mining industry. Earlier in his career as a colliery manager, he introduced many safety innovations in mines in the Nottinghamshire coal fields. In 1905, when he was General Mine Manager at Hucknall Collieries, he installed the first exhaust steam turbo-alternator generator to be used in a British mine, and in 1908 added a booster motor generator and equalising battery charging system, a combination unique in the history of engineering development. At the time it was the

***Above left:*** *Monica Maurice and Paul Roedel, who was the works manager in a picture dating from March 1939.* ***Below:*** *Outside the Saxon Road works, Spring 1938.*

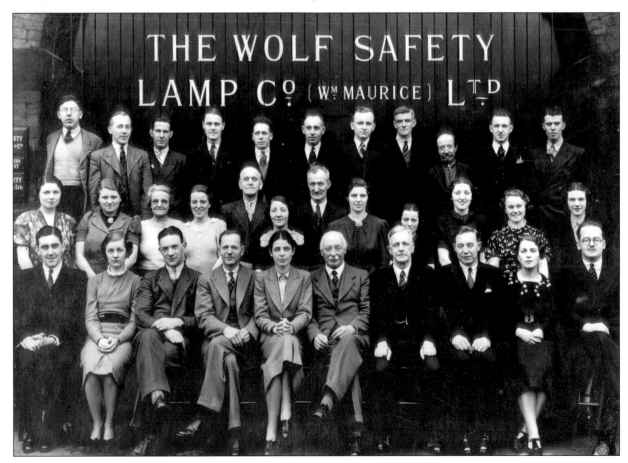

only example of its kind in the world. He was also the first to develop the thin coal seams of the Leen Valley Colliery, and the first to make use of electric coal-cutters in the area. He passionately believed that electricity, both for lighting and machinery, was the only way forward for the future development of the safety and efficiency of coal mining production. His conviction was such that, together with like minded colleagues, he co-founded the Association of Mining Electrical Engineers and was elected first president.

William Maurice was born in Macclesfield in 1872 and originally embarked upon a career in chemistry and metal-lurgy, but in 1890 he joined John Davis & Son of Derby as an articled electrical engineering student. He played an active roll in the installation of some of the earliest mining electrical plants in the country and acquired his first practical knowledge of lamp manufacturing. In 1892-93 he installed electrical equipment in the mines at Kimberley in South Africa on behalf of Davis of Derby. In 1894 he was appointed electrical engineer at Swanwick Collieries, Alfreton and subsequently became assistant to the manager, Mr J W Eardley, under whom he qualified as a

colliery manager. By 1899, he had obtained his Colliery Manager's certificate and was appointed manager of the Babbington Coal Company's Tibshelf New Colliery where he remained until 1903 before moving to Hucknall.

It was while he was at Hucknall that he married Helen Laura Wheeler, whose family were in the wine importing trade and were of considerable means. Monica, the first of three daughters was born at The Elms, Hucknall in 1908 followed by Cynthia a year later and Pauline in 1914, by which time the family were established in Sheffield. They lived firstly at Ridgeway, then Mushroom Lane, but in 1920, William Maurice purchased a 20 year lease on Park Grange, part of the Norfolk estates on the hillside above Farm Lane and Granville Road, long since demolished for replacement with high-rise flats. PG, as it was affection-ately known by friends and family, was a large Victorian mansion house set in acres of farmland with panoramic views of the City. It was a happy and informative household for the three young girls, brought up by

*Above:* *The new, clean, open and well-lit spaces of the Saxon Road works in 1934.*

accomplished and intellectual parents, hosting many parties, gatherings and musical evenings, as well as entertaining celebrated house guests, throughout the 1920s and 1930s.

This era was the heyday for William Maurice and the Company. He was a man of many parts, had an inventive mind and was an avid collector of art and literature of the period. He was also a natural orator and a gifted writer. Many of his technical papers were published in the

Institute of Mining Engineers Journal and over 60 papers, articles and learned comments have been attributed to him.

He was exceptionally well read and built an impressive library of first editions by contemporary authors, some of whom he knew. Over the years he collected and commis-

**Above:** *An apprentice drilling the top ring holder for lamps, Saxon Road works in 1934.*

sioned paintings, prints and drawings on mining subjects, some by major German Expressionist artists. He was also fascinated by the culture and traditions of miners, as referred to and recorded in prose, poetry and song. Over years 1924 to 1942, he collected together a significant amount of material from which he compiled a 'Pitman's Anthology', but due to lack of contemporary appeal it was never published. It is planned to publish this unique and informative collection in the future. William Maurice also recognised the value of catalogues, promotions and trade marks, and his approach to this subject was very progressive for the day.

The wolf's head emblem, facing ahead, first registered as a trade mark by the Leeds Company, was redesigned for the catalogue of 1914, but in the 1920s and up to 1936, the design reverted back to the Friemann & Wolf emblem of the wolf's head in a circle, lamp in mouth, facing to the left. With the new era of the Model Factory on line in 1935, the wolf's head was redesigned, this time facing to the right, used up to 1959. From 1960 to the early 1980, the Company logo was taken from a brass casting of a wolf's head, face on, but without a lamp in its mouth. From then, until the current logo, a modernised version of the pre-war Wolf was used. The new logo echoes something of the tradition of all these emblems, but with the head tilted upwards, as though scenting the air for new opportunities. The style of graphics, lettering and design of all these catalogues is a faithful reflection of the period in which they were designed, and serve as endorsements of the quality of all The Wolf Safety Lamp Company products and services, past and present.

The Company, which also embraced William Maurice's Federation Lamp Co. Ltd., had since grown from that of a one man business with a few helpers, run initially from Boston Street in 1911, to a workshop in the outbuildings of the family home at 358 Mushroom Lane, Western Park, then to the Star Works in Young Street in 1920, relocating to South Street, Park, behind the Sheffield Midland Railway Station from 1923. Throughout the 1920s, the Company had a manufacturing agreement with another of the major German lamp maker, Concordia (CEAG) of Dortmund, and also rented a small London office at 16a John Street in London. During these early days William Maurice registered 10 patented improvements to acetylene, flame and air turbo safety mining lamps. A further indicator of William Maurice's liberal attitude, rare in the realms of engineering at that time, was that his three daughters were educated at Bedales, a progressive co-educational boarding school in Hampshire, where Monica became head girl in 1926.

After school she studied languages at the Sorbonne in Paris, where she made many lifelong friends, and then Engineering at Hamburg University. Her original intention was to become a dress designer and although her passion for clothes remained with her throughout her life, she changed to engineering with the realisation that no-one else in the family would succeed her father. In February 1930, Monica Maurice joined the Company, becoming a director of the newly formed Hiring Company in 1932, formally Maurice's own Federation Lamp Company, and a director of The Wolf Safety Lamp Co. in 1934. This was the beginning of a career which lasted until her retirement in 1992, a period of more than sixty years.

1933 was a momentous year for the Company, with the purchase of the industrial site still occupied today, known as Saxon Road Works in Heeley, overlooking the former site of Heeley station and river Sheaf. With the appointment of the head of architecture at Sheffield University, Prof. Stephen Welsh, incidentally a lifelong friend of John Betjamin, and the experienced input of works manager Paul Roedel, formally of Friemann & Wolf, the buildings were completely reconstructed and installed with new electrically operated machinery, the first in Sheffield, creating a Model Factory. The first floor offices

***Above:*** *Three examples of the wolf's head logos used by the company.*

were also reconstructed and supplied with Pilkington tiled fireplaces, new modern office furniture and filing systems, commissioned in oak and ebony with steel frame and leather upholstered chairs, all to Monica Maurice's own designs. The entire building was equipped with an internal telephone system, central heating through hot water pipes and maximised the use of daylight in the offices and on the factory floor. On each first floor windowsill was a carefully tended window box full of colourful flowers, in contrast to the drab, dirty and smoky atmosphere that enveloped most major cities of the day.

By 1934, with an increased work force, the new factory was in full production, manufacturing a range of safety lamps as broad and diverse as any in Britain. Two years later, Monica Maurice organised a conference for the Women's Engineering Society at Sheffield University, which included a tour of The Wolf Safety Lamp Company's Model Factory of the New Electric Age. That year, Mrs J A Mollison, better known as Amy Johnson, the world famous aviator, was president of the

Society. Monica was not only a talented organiser but a gifted and natural linguist, fluent in French and German. She had studied office management before embarking on her training with the Company and the former parent Company in Saxony. Throughout the 1930s she continued with regular visits to Germany, but in 1939 she had some difficulty in returning home before war was declared. On a number of occasions she presented papers on her father's behalf, in French, to the Congres International des Mines in Liege and at a later date, in German, at similar conferences held in Berlin and Karlsruhe. Like her father, she was also an active member of the Institute of Mining Engineers and AMEMME, (later to incorporate Mining Mechanical Engineers), and in due course was elected a member of the Institute of Electrical Engineers (IEE), and a fellow of the Institute of Quality Assurance.

**Above left:** *A catalogue from 1914.*
**Top:** *A demonstration of the Wolf Safety Lamp range to lamp room managers.*

and her sisters regularly attended, with eligible young men, throughout the 1930s. Many of her dresses and hats from that period, some commissioned from makers such as Motley, who made her red wedding dress, are now in the collection of the Victoria & Albert Museum. George Brough of Motorcycle fame, gave her the occasional drive in the Works supercharged Brough Superior hill climbing car, known as the 'Girl Pat'. Post-war, she ran a Brough Superior, as did her husband, followed by a Mark VI Bentley in which she delivered and collected her three children to and from boarding school in Hampshire. Latterly she ran an ex-works Aston Martin with primrose yellow paint work which, with its open exhausts, could be heard long before it was seen!

In her spare time she learned to fly and flew various Blackburn aircraft from the Yorkshire Flying Club at Sherburn in Elmet, often with Joy Davison the well known aviator and aerial photographer. The story goes that they would sometimes race there and back from Park Grange, Monica in her chain gang Fraser Nash, Joy being in her faster but less nimble Isotta Fraschini. The Fraser Nash gaining a substantial lead on the initial twisty roads, only to be reduced on the Great North Road by the much more powerful Italian machine, arriving at the same time! Monica's zeal for cars was almost matched with that for fashion dresses, hats, dances and tennis parties which she

In 1938 she met Canadian doctor, Arthur Jackson at a tennis party, and after a whirlwind romance they were married in the Chapel on the Bridge in Rotherham. They settled down to domestic life at Ash Croft on the Fitzwilliam Estate in Wentworth village, but there was

***Above left:*** *Monica with her chain-gang Fraser Nash in 1935.* ***Below:*** *The Women's Engineering Society at Wolf's premises in 1936. Monica Maurice is left of centre and Amy Johnson is right of centre.*

never any question of her giving up her career. Even so, she was devoted to her family and the household was ultra-efficiently managed with capable local help, readily available in those days.

Two years later, Arthur Jackson purchased a General Medical Practice in Woodhouse on the east side of Sheffield and the family moved into Newton Croft, a Georgian House in Chapel Street in the centre of the village, now a retirement home. It was a small friendly mining community, where both were active in local events and were often called upon for advice. Monica was quick to recognise those living locally who had skills in making clothes and house furnishings and, in the Maurice tradition, commissioned much from the village over the years. Not surprisingly, some of the Company's newly recruited work force lived in Woodhouse and Bob Graves, a much respected local Scout Master, ran a 'taxi' service to and from Saxon Road in his converted army ambulance for many years. Arthur Jackson retired in 1972 and he and Monica moved to the tranquil Derbyshire village of Ashford in the Water near Bakewell, where they enjoyed regular visits of their children and grandchildren in their latter years.

1943, the younger, John, now runs the company. In pre-war days on visits to Germany she had developed a very special friendship with the Wolf family, and in particular Carl Wolf's daughter Erika and son Paul, who then ran the Company. She often stayed with them at their country house at Schonsee, near Weiden by the Czech border. When she was invited in 1947 to participate in a British Intelligence Objectives Sub-committee survey team to assess the war damage and reclamation of the German battery industry, she leaped at the opportunity. With the rank of full Colonel heading a team of six engineers, with two drivers and cars, they covered dozens of sites in all four occupied zones in just six weeks. During this visit she re-met her close friend Erika, but in much changed and sad circumstances. Her notes, reports and personal diary of this experience are a part of the Company archive and may well be published one of these days.

**Above left:** *Celebrations with the staff of the Company on Monica's 50 years with Wolf Safety - 1980.* **Above:** *William Maurice's Federation Lamp Company stand at an exhibition in Cardiff in the 1920s.* **Below:** *Wolf's stand at the National Coalboard Exhibition in Wrexham between February and March 1951.*

During the war years, the Company continued making miners lamps for the 'Bevin Boys', but as a further part of the war effort they produced aircraft fuel pumps. During this period, Monica served on a number of British Standards Committees, including one for standardising screw threads, recounting the trials and tribulations during the latter part of the war, in dealing with the Russians. Her daughter was born in 1941 and twin sons in

The 1950s was about rebuilding lost markets, and the Company's survival entailed a combination of orders from the National Coal Board and the export of safety lamps, in particular to the mines in South Africa and South America. With the death of William Maurice in 1951, it was crucial that there was an enthusiastic and capable team working with Monica. Great credit has to be made to the loyalty of the work force and management in those difficult days, many of whom spent their entire working life with the Company.

With the rapid decline of the coal industry, the two key areas of expansion in the next two decades lay in contracts with all the major oil tanker fleets for the much improved air turbo lamp, and the development of the new revolutionary Wolflite Handlamp, a rechargeable safety lamp made of engineering plastics, designed specifically for the emerging oil and gas industries.

The pattern of trading and commerce was also changing, with specialist distributors and agents being appointed throughout the world. Today, the Company's top international distributors, many established for twenty years or more, account for a significant part of its turnover. In particular are companies such as Nor Marine of Oslo, Wah Hong of Singapore, and Safety Lamp of Houston.

In 1970, Tom Fallon, an avid American collector of mining lamps, called on Monica Maurice for advice about a book he was planning to write on the history of mining lamps. Within an hour into the discussion

he had shelved the project as he realised how relatively little he knew about the subject. But two years later, in response to letters from Wolf Safety to various US contacts seeking agencies in North America, a telegram was received by return from Tom which read; 'I have just today registered Safety Lamp of Houston and hopefully I am now your first main agent in North America'. That was the start of a long and fruitful relationship that exists to this day. By the 1980s, Groupe Leader, was appointed for the French market and more recently appointed was Technokontroll, for the marketing of Wolf Safety products in Switzerland.

Today there is a new team and work force supporting the third and fourth generation of the family, just as enthusiastic and dedicated as the those of decades ago. With the development of new technology, the commitment to a dedicated research and development programme, the future of The Wolf Safety Lamp Co. of Sheffield looks very bright indeed. On looking back, one has to reflect on the greatest moments and achievements in the history of the Company. Without a doubt it has to be when Monica Maurice, known throughout Sheffield, the coal fields and the world of safety engineering as 'The lady of the Lamp', was presented with the OBE by HM The Queen in 1975. This great tribute was awarded to her in recognition of her outstanding contribution and dedication to safety in mining and industry.

*Copyright: William Jackson July 2000*

**Above left:** *Monica Maurice with Tom Fallon of Safety Lamp of Houston at the Magpie Mine, May 1975.*
**Above right:** *Monica Maurice with her OBE, with her husband, Arthur Jackson, and their daughter, Willa and son, John, in 1975.*
**Right:** *John Jackson outside the Saxon Road works after complete refurbishment in 1993, pictured here with the last Wolf Miner's Lamp.*

# Memorable moments

**This page:** Thousands of pounds worth of damage was caused, and scores of families were made homeless across 40 square miles when storms lashed South Yorkshire at the beginning of July 1958. In a few short hours the River Sheaf rose an incredible 14 ft, and unable to cope with the force of the torrent, the river banks burst and a wall of water surged into the surrounding streets. The parapet of the road bridge at Totley Brook was completely swept away, followed by a street lamp and a foot-bridge; cars were picked up like toys and smashed against buildings, and floodwater poured into nearby homes.

Clyde Road, Heeley, was one of the worst hit by the pent up force of the flood water *(top)*. One family in Clyde Road was taken unawares as their back door simply burst open and flood water surged into their home, picking up items of furniture as it went. The

upper floors were the only answer as people realised that they were trapped in their homes, and the bedrooms became a refuge for entire families. When the flood water eventually subsided, wet, hungry and mud spattered people ventured out to assess the damage. Indoors, their carpets and linoleum were covered with a thick layer of silt and mud; wallpaper was stained with dirty tide marks which showed just how high the water had reached, while television sets, sideboards, tables and three piece suites were completely ruined.

Our photographs reveal a little of what lay outside, where the road was still awash with mud and debris - and the hard-pressed fire brigade was called upon to pump away hundreds of gallons of flood water that had turned roads into lakes. Neighbours helped each other to drag their soggy possessions out on to the pavements. It was all too much for some of the children who lived in the area; the camera has caught a look of sad bewilderment on the face of one little girl. What clothes and toys did she lose in that traumatic night, we wonder?

It was back in 1937 when an enterprising photographer snapped this busy scene in the Haymarket from the Brightside and Carbrook Co-op (destined, sadly, to be destroyed a few years later in the Blitz). The date was 22nd May, and on the left of the photograph we can see the red, white and blue garlands and bunting still hanging from the buildings, celebrating the coronation of King George VI. The coronation itself was held on 12th May 1937 - and though the new King was welcomed by his subjects, things were quite different from was the original plan. Britain had expected Edward VIII to reign after the death of his father King George V. In the event, the monarch being crowned was Edward's younger brother Albert, Duke of York. He had been hurled unexpectedly into the kingship he had not been trained for when his older brother, who had been king for a mere 325 days, renounced the throne on 10 December 1936 for American divorcee Wallis Simpson, 'the woman I love.' The new King had never seen a state paper in his life - but he rose to the challenge, squared his shoulders, and adopted the title of George VI. King George VI went on to take his place as perhaps Britain's most well loved monarch.

**This page:** It was 2nd July 1958 - the height of the British summer time - and though the odd thunderstorm could be expected, the catastrophic effects of this particular storm caught South Yorkshire unawares. As the River Sheaf burst its banks in the night of disastrous flooding (and with further heavy rain forecast), many Sheffield families had to abandon their homes to the water and spend the night in hastily arranged reception centres. In some areas, thousands of gallons of water surged through streets and gardens, sweeping away garden sheds, greenhouses and garages - some complete with cars - and uprooting trees . One elderly lady was warned by neighbours in the nick of time before her cottage in Yarborough Road crumbled under the onslaught and fell into the river. In other places, the deadly waters rose silently around homes in the darkness, and only a night-time peep through the window revealed flood water lapping at the bedroom windowsills. There were many narrow escapes that night, but sadly a number of pets fell victim to the flood. When daylight came the full extent of the damage was revealed. A number of families were left homeless, without food, and with only the clothes they were wearing, and many of them found refuge in Fir Vale Infirmary. At last the mopping up operations began, and the first thing to do was to drag ruined furniture out into the street so that walls and floors could be dried and cleaned - though the scum of smelly mud which coated everything was messy to deal with and difficult to get rid of. The Women's Voluntary Service, as it was then, and the Sheffield Lions Club, were just two of the organisations which rolled up their sleeves and came to the rescue. Dry clothing was a priority, and an urgent appeal went out for help. Help of a different kind came from the Sheffield and District Rabbit Keepers' Association, who offered to replace all the pet rabbits which had been lost in the flood. Help of any kind was greatly appreciated by those who had lost all their treasured possessions in the worst floods in 30 years.

**This page:** Sheffield turned out in full force to welcome King George VI and Queen Elizabeth - our Queen's parents - when they visited the city on 25th September 1945. In Broomhill hundreds of people lined the route of the royal couple's procession, and eager anticipation can be seen on every face in this revealing photograph *(above)*. Union Jacks hang from upper windows - and when the royal car arrives, the same windows will no doubt give a few lucky people a convenient grand-stand view! The crowds were on the whole good tempered, but all the same the event put a strain on the police, who had trouble keeping people from

pushing past the barriers to get as near to the King and Queen as they could. One can hardly blame them - they simply loved the royal couple, who during the war had showed great courage by staying on in England when they could have been evacuated to safety. They insisted that they be treated like everyone else, even to wartime rationing, and the Queen was almost relieved when Buckingham Palace was bombed. She felt that she could now identify with his people and look them in the face! The King and Queen's last visit to Sheffield had been in January 1941, when they had visited the city to comfort people who had lost everything in the bombing raids, and the people of Sheffield felt that they knew these royals personally. Fortunately, the weather was fine and the hood of the King and Queen's limousine was let down, giving the crowds a good view of the royal couple *(top)*. The purpose of their visit was to open the new Ladybower Reservoir (which had actually been planned 46 years earlier), where King George ceremonially turned a wheel, sending water through the outlet valves. The 504 acre reservoir, which would supply water to Nottingham, Leicester and Derby as well as Sheffield, could hold up to 6,300,000,000 gallons.

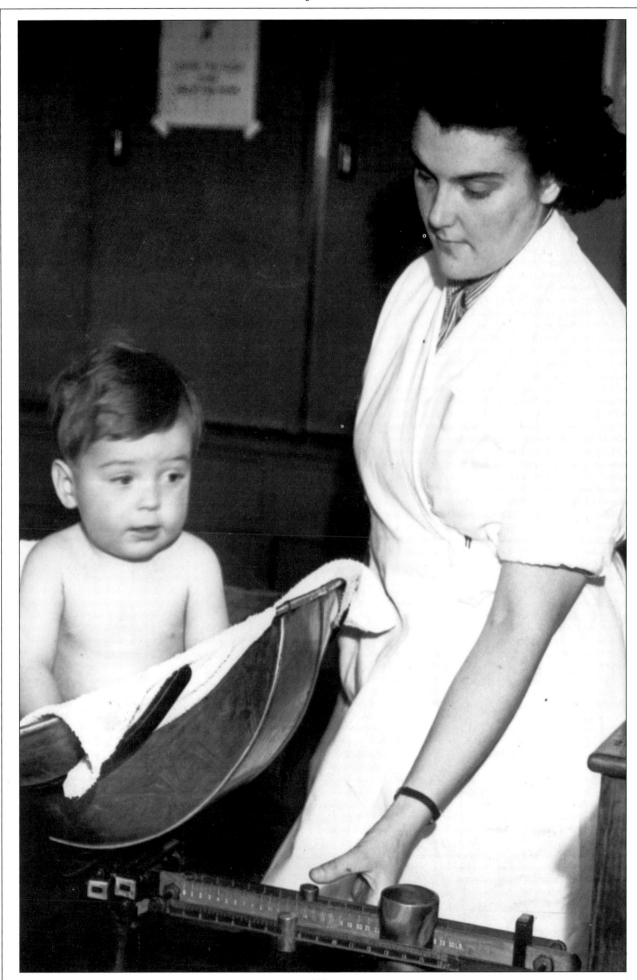

**Both pages:** It was possibly the acute wartime shortages of food and supplies which made doctors, health workers and mothers alike very aware of the health of the new generation, and children were carefully weighed, measured and immunised against the illnesses that had at one time meant disfigurement or even death *(facing page)*. A vaccine for polio, the scourge of former years which left behind its terrible mark of wasted and useless limbs, only came later, however. American scientist Jonas Edward Salk developed a vaccine in 1955, and an oral vaccine was produced in 1960. The vaccines brought the dreaded disease under control and today polio is rarely seen. On a day to day basis, vitamins were vital to the health of children, and long before the advent of the cod liver oil capsule, the recommended spoonful of cod liver oil was administered to the youngest children every day in schools and nurseries around the country during the 1940s. Children might have screwed up their noses at the fishy taste, but the nourishing cod liver oil went a long way towards keeping them healthy. The vitamin-packed orange juice was far more palatable, and artful mothers would often use the orange juice as a bribe: no cod liver oil, no orange juice. Following hard on the heels of the oil, the juice took away the distinctive taste that was disliked by so many children. Ante-natal clinics did all

they could to check on the diet, blood pressure and vitamin intake of mothers to be; our carefully posed photograph, taken in a Sheffield ante-natal clinic in the 1930s, records at least the clean-liness and tidiness that was to their great credit *(bottom)*. And when the tiny new Sheffield citizen finally arrived, there were health visitors to pay friendly calls on families in their homes to check on the health and happiness of mothers and babies *(left)*. National Dried Milk for babies was also made available to mothers, and before today's push towards natural feeding NDM was for decades very much in vogue. We need to remember that at the time of these photographs the National Health service did not exist, and in fact the NHS only came into operation after World War II in July 1948.

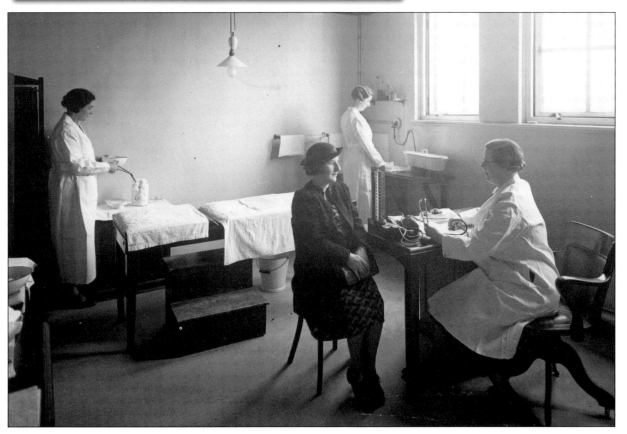

When women tie scarves around their hair, roll up their sleeves and bring out the buckets, mops and cleaning cloths, it spells curtains for any dirt and grime that happens to be around. Not a crisp bag, not a sweet wrapper - not even a spent match - lie around Darnall railway station to mar its smart appearance; the posts have been whitewashed, the seats dusted, and any brave dandelion or daisy that has dared to raise its head among the colourful blooms in the flowerbeds has been ruthlessly uprooted. And as the photographer records the occasion for posterity, even the Darnall Station sign is being treated to a final polish. If readers are wondering what prompted such a level of care and attention we can reveal that these ladies had not simply got out their brooms and dusters because they enjoyed the exercise! The year was 1962, and final preparations were being made for the 'Best Kept Station' competition. The ladies' loving care paid off, as Darnall, of course, very deservedly ran away with the award.

# The People's War

L ooking extremely fetching in dungarees and tin hats, the Central Library staff get together for a group photograph. This was 1940, and the buckets and stirrup pumps placed near them on the library roof hint at the fact that the girls were going through their ARP training at the time. The 16-strong group is 100 per cent female - not unusual for wartime, as many of their husbands, sweethearts and brothers had already joined up, left their jobs, and gone to war. As they had in the previous war, women took over their jobs in machine shops and engineering factories, turning out armaments and aeroplane parts,

driving buses and lorries - in fact doing most kinds of work that had always been looked on as 'jobs for the boys'. Housewives across the country discovered talents and abilities they never knew they had, and developed skills which surprised even themselves. The second world war was to change the way of life for hundreds of men and women, turning generations of tradition upside down. Volunteers of both sexes were needed to fulfil all kinds of duties, whether it was in Air Raid Prevention, as these young ladies, the Women's Land Army, the WVS, the evacuation service, or in one of the countless other voluntary services.

**Above:** Looking very smart, the York & Lancaster Regiment 69 West Riding Home Guard C-Company stand to attention for inspection. This was the first parade of a Sheffield Home Guard Unit; the men were a credit to the city, and a photographer was present to record the event for posterity. When war broke out in 1939, Sir Anthony Eden, the Secretary of State for War, made a radio appeal for men outside military age to volunteer for membership of the LDV to defend their country in the event of Nazi invasion. Teenagers of 17 and able-bodied senior citizens all rushed to put their names down; many of these young men and women would later volunteer for one of the services (though conscription was already in the pipeline), and most of the senior citizens had already served King and country in the first world war. Old or young, every member of the LDV was prepared to do his or her bit for Britain. At the beginning of the war, broom handles were typical of the type of 'weapon' the new force had to made do with. They had to improvise, and men had to rely on sticks and on the odd few shotguns which had been handed in.

**Above right:** It's 'Eyes left!' as a unit of the York and Lancaster Home Guard Regiment march past the saluting base in front of the Town Hall back in 1940. As many readers will remember, military parades were to become an accepted part of life during the second world war, and were a real morale-booster. Remember the far-off beat of the drum which brought us all scurrying out of our houses and down the street to watch the soldiers march by to the rhythm of the rousing bands? The parades undoubtedly made the average person in the street feel in touch with the military and the progress of the war. The Home Guard might have been an amateur force, but they were very well organised. As German bombers wrought havoc in Bristol, Coventry and Birmingham, the people of Sheffield, heart of Britain's steel manufacture, braced themselves for the inevitable; the Luftwaffe would surely come - but when? Observation was a key role of the Home Guard, and fire watching was seen as a vital job which could save important factories and commercial premises from destruction. Invasion was a real fear during the early 1940s, and here, too the Home Guard played their part. If parachutes were seen landing, local church bells would be rung to summon the unpaid volunteers from their normal jobs of work (and compensation would be made for any loss of wages caused by a call to action stations).

The inevitable knot of spectators gather to watch as the RAF prepare to inflate their barrage balloon on Crookemoor Recreation Ground, one of the 72 sites which had been earmarked for these all important defences during World War II. Note the gas cylinders piled in readiness on the trailer behind the lorry, most probably containing helium. Parks and other areas of open land made ideal sites for the balloons, which were an effective obstacle to the kind of dive bombing raids sometimes made by the enemy. The city clocked up a total of 130 air raid alerts during the war, but it was December 1940 when Sheffield's defences were taxed to the limit. Everyone had done their bit, but the barrage balloons, fire watchers, anti-aircraft guns and fire fighters were not sufficient to save the city from widespread death and destruction. Every one of the 72 barrage balloons was up and flying during the blitz, and even though 47 of them were damaged in the raids, they were immediately repaired and within 12 hours were back on duty. Bad weather was the main enemy of the balloons; the cables could become brittle and would occasionally snap as the balloons were set free, and on frosty nights the balloons themselves were inclined to ice up and fall from the sky.

**Bottom:** An unbelievable crowd of 20,000 turned out to cheer Prime Minister Winston Churchill when he visited Sheffield on 8th November 1941. He was able to promise little other than 'blood, sweat and tears', but his stirring speeches inspired the people of Britain in general and Sheffield in particular, and they were with him all the way. As his limousine swept through the city streets, old and young alike cheered him on as he waved his stick, his bowler hat and his big cigar, returning his famous 'V for Victory' sign. Outside the Town Hall vast crowds gathered, yelling, waving, cheering - then listening with respect as he spoke into the microphone, sympathising with the people of Sheffield and berating Adolf Hitler and his policies. After all the city had gone through at the hands of the Luftwaffe, Sheffield needed all the encouragement that the great wartime leader had to give - and they loved him. It was Churchill's strong leadership which took the country through the bitter years of loss and hardship to decisive victory - and perhaps without it, Britain would have surrendered to Hitler. A great soldier, statesman, author and artist, Winston Churchill died in 1965 at the age of 90.

**Right:** On the 12th December 1940 the air raid sirens sounded across Sheffield, signalling a long night of untold destruction as German bombs rained down on the city for hour after hour. In the comparative safety of their Anderson shelters, or huddled together beneath the stairs - the strongest part of the house - families listened fearfully as the bombs struck. Where were the bombs falling? What would they find when daylight dawned and they set off to work? Would their workplace have been left standing? Wearily, the workers caught buses when and where they could, as many of the normal routes were blocked, then picked their way through the scattered bricks and rubble towards their factories, offices and shops. Those who worked at C&A Modes Ltd in High Street found this heartbreaking sight awaiting them on their arrival - little remained of the handsome fashion store apart from a smouldering mass of twisted steel girders. Opened in 1932, the building had been built a mere eight years earlier on the site of the old Fitzalan Market. Next door, the Burtons building on the corner of Angel Street was ruined - as were virtually all the buildings on that side of High Street. Strangely, there was little damage done to the premises opposite.

# Wheels of time

I t's just not his day, is it? Well, how many of these jay-walking pedestrians are taking notice of the lone police officer on point duty in Fargate? The neglect was enough to give him a complex! The reason for the huge crowds and air of suppressed excitement seems to have been Cole Brothers sale - the whole world appears to be beating a path to their door. A well placed sign above the entrance reads '1847 - 1930 - wonderful birthday offers in every department', and though 83 years seems an odd number of years to turn into a special celebration the bargains are welcome all the same,

and we can read a definite air of purpose into the confident stride of these potential customers. The fashions of 1930 are worth drawing attention to, from the cloche hat of the mother shepherding her toddler across the road to the gent in front of her; his plus fours, though respectable enough, would have made him a rare bird in Sheffield city centre. A terrifying barrage of trams has turned Fargate into an obstacle course which makes us all the more thankful that present day planning has created a vehicle-free pedestrianised area, while High Street and Church Street are part of our one-way system.

**Above:** Bus stations and railway stations go together like fish and chips or cheese and wine - but it is surprising how many cities around Britain have separated these two means of transport by a ten or fifteen minute walk. Fine for taxi drivers, though not good for holiday-makers carrying a couple of heavy suitcases and wheeling a baby buggy. Sheffield, however, is different. Travellers arriving by train had only to walk a short distance from the Midland Station to the bus station in Pond Street. So sensible! The bus station was actually planned before the second world war, and by the mid 1950s it was ready for a few renovations. Cold, draughty and damp, those open shelters gave little protection from winter winds and driving rain! In 1956 the bus station received a facelift, which added escalators and bridges to the nearby shops. The 1990s brought further modernisation to Sheffield's bus station, and the railway station - which itself underwent tasteful renovations - was linked to the bus station by a covered walkway.

**Below:** Car number 182 may not have been the 'school special' (was there such a thing back in 1956?), but a good number of schoolchildren are among the passengers about to board this Meadowhead tram. Is it imagination, or were children on their way to school much better behaved back then than some of today's youngsters? They were certainly noisy and without a doubt often cheeky, but their cheek lacked the aggression that all too often prompts fights and vandalism. These lively youngsters chat cheerfully to the tram driver before boarding car number 182 which in 1956 was nearing the end of its lifespan. The car first came into service in 1934 and had carried the people of Sheffield around the city for more than twenty years when it was finally scrapped in 1957, three years before the last of the old trams ran in Sheffield. The Meadowhead route took passengers right to the Sheffield boundary, just about as far as the city's trams went.

**Below:** By 1950, the date of this photograph, Sheffielders had grown used to the empty spaces and derelict buildings which were the legacy of the Nazi bombing raids made 10 years earlier. Rebuilding was going ahead, of course, but strict building restrictions meant that these things took time. This particular empty space, viewed from a vantage point above the Haymarket, had once been occupied by the Brightside and Carbrook Co-op in Exchange Street. A new co-op had already been built on the corner of Angel Street and Castle Street, and long queues formed outside the new store on the day of their grand opening in 1950. It was a one-storey building, and other departments were added over the years. Today, Castle Market occupies part of this empty site. The new market - first begun in 1930 - opened in 1962, and became hugely popular with the shopping public. At the time of our photograph, however, many of Sheffield's bomb sites were used for advertising hoardings and parking cars. The attractions of Belle Vue, near Manchester, were being advertised in our photograph. Many of its facilities had closed during the war, but Belle Vue rapidly regained popularity and during the post war boom between the mid 1940s and early 1950s, literally millions converged upon the pleasure grounds.

**Bottom:** The sky is overcast and the road surface gleams with 'spits and spots' of rain in this post war view of Fargate. The photographer has captured an interesting variety of vehicles, from the faithful old trams in the background to the sporty convertible on the left. Caudles, whose van can be seen driving away from the camera, has long been a well-known Sheffield removals firm. Some kind of activity involving a length of electricity cable is taking place atop the lorry behind

the convertible, though unfortunately we cannot detect exactly what these two men are doing. The date of the photograph is 1948, and younger readers will be interested to spot Cook's Travel Services on the left, a long established firm who occupy the same premises today. Thomas Cook, the grandson of a Baptist minister, was a great supporter of the temperance movement; he organised his first excursion in 1841 - a temperance occasion, of course - from Leicester to Loughborough, with tea and a brass band included in the price. Cook invented the package tour, always personally making an exploratory trip beforehand to check on the cafes and restaurants in the area and the kind of attractions that might interest travellers.

**Both pages:** How many readers still have the pennies they laid on the tramlines to be bent by the wheels of Sheffield's last tram? It would be interesting to know just how many of these novel souvenirs still lie forgotten in drawers and boxes around the city! The last of the old trams signalled the end of an era, but older people will never forget boarding their tram on the way home after a long day's work. Sheffield's tramway services never really recovered after World War II, when no fewer than 14 tramcars were destroyed by enemy bombing and the fires that followed. Coupled with this, the centre of the city was hardly ideal for operating a tramway system - the busy section that lay between Lady's Bridge and Fitzalan Square was too narrow to take the increasing numbers of motor vehicles as well as trams. By the mid 1950s the days of the tram were numbered. A week of celebration preceded the demise of the tramway; remember the beautifully decorated and illuminated 1907 tram car which ran around the city that week? The open topped tram was specially painted in the black and yellow livery used by the stage coach service between Sheffield and London back in 1760. The 8th October was designated as the last day of Sheffield trams, and to say that

the day was rather wet would be understating the torrential downpour which was as memorable as the last tram! At six o'clock in the evening the procession of 15 trams left the depot at Tenter Street - and the pouring rain did not stop people from turning out in their thousands to see them off. Cheering and waving, they watched as the procession passed by, with Sheffield's official 'last tram', car number 510, bringing up the rear. In the Town Hall Square, floodlit for the occasion, the Transport Band played 'Auld Lang Syne', and the vast crowd joined in the singing as a farewell wreath was placed on the old car's front bumper.

Tinsley tramshed (ironically, Sheffield Bus Museum today) lay just across the road from Thomas Ward's scrapyard, and it was a simple matter to dispatch the old trams to their final destination. A last photograph recorded the scene as the first cars stand in line awaiting their fate *(left)*. Did any of these officials and workers standing around feel just a touch of sadness now that the fate of the faithful old trams was signed and sealed? Before long, out came the welding torches and car number 536 was sent on its last journey to that great tramshed in the sky.... A few trams escaped the slaughter and were sent to Crich tramway museum; one which had already been despatched to the scrapyard had a very narrow escape. Sheffield, of course, made history as the last industrial city in England to run a tram service. Since then, of course, the South Yorkshire Supertram has added its own flavour to the city streetscene.

Refuse collecting has never been thought of as the most pleasant job in the world, but alongside the task of these two 'bin men', today's refuse collectors have never had it so good! In a rather nice city suburb - exact location unknown - rubbish is being disposed of in a way which is quite unfamiliar to us today as two brave blokes have a close encounter with cinders, ash, dirt and smells. Walk around the house, pick up the rubbish, carry the galvanised containers back to the cart, then climb up the ladder and tip it in. And then do it all again...and again. At some stage in the proceedings, they have picked up and loaded a rather unpleasant old mattress. It all went with the job. A third member of the team has been assigned a slightly better duty as the driver of Dustcart Number 64 - a very strange vehicle. How much did it weigh, we wonder? Its solid tyres and massive bulk no doubt made it a beast to drive and gave its passenger a bumpy and uncomfortable ride. Contrast all this with the marvellous vehicles and their mechanical crushers which the City of Sheffield's Cleansing Department has today, and the gloves, protective clothing, plastic bags and special bins. How times have changed! The photograph was taken around 1940.

# Making a living

**A** **bove:** It may take readers a minute or two to orientate themselves and pinpoint the exact location of this view from April 1965, taken at the junction of Surrey Street and Tudor Street. Tudor Street no longer exists today as the entire block of buildings nearest the camera was demolished (and along with it the shop on the corner, the premises of Jenkinson, Marshall & Co) to make way for the building of Tudor Square. The building which stands roughly a third of the way along the row was eventually to form the corner of Tudor Square and is today the Information Office. Memorable vehicles of the day add interest to the scene, with a Vauxhall Cresta turning right into Surrey Street from Tudor Street, and a rather nice Hillman Minx Mark II in the right foreground. The Central Library and Graves Art Gallery lie off-picture to the right; the facility has been a valuable part of the city's life since it was opened by the Duchess of York in 1934, three years before she became Queen. Her husband, Prince Albert (our Queen's father, who later became King George VI), was to have performed the ceremony but was unable to keep the appointment because of illness. Off to the left, standing slightly taller than the terrace of houses, is the well respected Jeffie Bainbridge Children's Shelter.

This 1956 photograph awards us the rare privilege of viewing the City Council in session, and every eye is turned towards the camera, from the Lord Mayor to the members of the Council. Beneath a carved oak pediment bearing the Sheffield Coat of Arms sits the Lord Mayor, looking very imposing in his Chain of Office. Readers might be interested to know that the chain, weighing 32oz, cost £325 - a great extravagance when it was purchased in 1856, and is today worth around £5,000. The Council Chamber itself is as interesting to the people of Sheffield as these Council members.

The oak panelling and canopy behind the Lord Mayor's throne-like chair is a thing of beauty, while the bench in front of him bears a carving of two children ascending from the branches of a tree (dated 1896), with the watchword 'Work while it is day'. Little has changed in the room's appearance today, though one tradition at least has been established since the date of this photograph. The bell from Sheffield's last tram, car number 510, did not accompany the tram to the scrapyard, but was instead taken to the Council Chamber and is today used by the Lord Mayor to bring Council meetings to order. A very nice touch.

**Both pictures:** Jobs for the boys, jobs for the girls: segregation was the norm in the City Treasury - as it was everywhere else - in the 1950s. It was not until the country was in the grip of 1960s flower power that girls began to rebel against being relegated to the typewriter, the shop counter or the kitchen sink. Burning their bras (emotionally if not actually), they formed the women's liberation movement and in a male dominated society dared to demand equal rights and opportunities for women. Response to their demands was a long time coming, but the appointment of Margaret Thatcher as Britain's first female Prime Minister in 1979 was the turning point in many (though not all) occupations. In the City Treasury, it was the girls who worked on the punch card machines (working out the wages?), seen here in September 1959 *(bottom)*. A couple of male faces can be seen in the background, though we have to raise a sceptical eyebrow and wonder if they were there to supervise the ladies and make sure they got it right.... Readers who are too young to remember the almost obsolete punch card machines should know that this was an early form of data processing. Surprisingly, the earliest of these machines was developed as far back as the 1880s by Herman Hollerith for use in the US census.

Quite a different atmosphere prevailed in our second Treasury office, where men sat at their desks and got on with the really important stuff *(below left)*. Readers who themselves worked in offices during the 1950s will recognise the paraphernalia of the day with a wry smile: the adding machine - all important in those pre-PC days, when computers occupied entire rooms; the glass inkstands, hole punches, ledgers, box files, and rows of pens in the jacket pocket. All grist to the Treasury's mill. Interestingly, even close inspection of this photograph reveals but one telephone, near the column which tells us that the day's date was the 8th - and the receiver is off the hook. Obviously, these guys hated disturbance of any kind!

**Right:** The dark days of World War II still lay a number of years in the future when this view of the Endcliffe Grange police information room was captured back in 1933. A male police officer - presumably recording a reported crime - takes careful notes while his female colleague co-ordinates the response (is she making use of a tannoy system, we wonder?). The wall map of the Sheffield area, an illuminated display - and of course the vital telephone link - were all part of the modern technology of the day. Almost seven decades on, even lay persons whose knowledge of the mechanisms of police work is restricted to 'The Bill' or 'Heartbeat' will appreciate that things have changed more than a little since the days of good old 'PC 49'! Banks of computers, DNA matching, files on known criminals and their crimes, fast cars and police helicopters have replaced the methods which were more than adequate for the types of crime which were common in the 1930s, when in one year only four instances of 'taking away vehicles without the owner's consent' were recorded! Just before the second world war the city of Sheffield had a fleet of 15 police cars....

**Below:** We cannot tell a lie: working conditions in the Sheffield police operations room were, to say the least, Spartan. Our photograph is very revealing: while a number of staff members work on their feet below unshaded light bulbs, an officer in the foreground sits on a hard kitchen chair to do his paperwork on a folding card table. The flex of the one shaded light has been wound around a metal rod so that the bulb is positioned above the map; the walls badly need a coat of paint - and a forgotten teacup stands forlornly on the windowledge. In spite of the downside, however, each of these members of the Sheffield force appears to be totally absorbed in his task of solving crime and bringing the guilty to justice. Pins have been placed on the area map, presumably marking the places where a crime has taken place, while below, a set of photographs puts the crime into perspective - and hopefully point to the criminal. A date chalked on the blackboard indicates that this image was recorded on 10th January 1962, and it is interesting to note that although women were allowed to join the police force as far back as 1919, our photograph shows only one female police officer to six males.

vehicles were not required to go through an MOT road test (though one would have thought that taxis would have to prove their roadworthiness?). The Ministry of Transport introduced the Motor Vehicles (Tests) Regulations in 1959, though the new regulations at first affected only those cars which were 10 years old and over.

**Top:** Teaching young children to take care on the roads has always formed an important part of police work, and our happy snap, captured some time in the 1960s, records one of those vital road safety events. Acting out the theme with their pedal cars, scooters and dolls' prams made the demonstration fun and taught these youngsters - the drivers of the future - the meaning of various road signs and showed them just how to use pedestrian crossings. How many of our readers will recognise

**Above:** This 1950s photograph raises more questions than it answers. All we can say for certain is that these two police officers were 'checking a taxi'; the reason that lay behind the checkup remains open to the imagination - as does the reason why the occasion called for a photograph. Were these members of the Sheffield constabulary satisfying themselves that the vehicle was in good working order, or had they simply come to the rescue of a driver whose taxi had broken down? The policeman on the left would appear to know his way around the inside of a car, and, perhaps with a little advice from his superior officer, the 'hands on' part of the operation has been left to him. We can at least be reasonably sure that in those gentler days they would not have been searching for drugs! We have no firm date for the photograph, but during the 1950s

themselves as one of these children and will remember this road safety demonstration? Traffic accidents have been a growing problem since the 1920s and 30s - in fact, an unbelievable 120,000 people were killed on Britain's roads between the two world wars. The speed limit of 30mph in built up areas was introduced in 1934 with the Road Traffic Act; at the same time driving tests were made compulsory for the first time for new drivers. How strange to think that before then you could acquire a car and simply buy a licence to drive it! The Sheffield City Police, who were responsible for the road safety demonstration in the year of our photograph, became the South Yorkshire Constabulary in the early 1970s when the county boundaries changed and the Sheffield City Police amalgamated with Doncaster, Rotherham and Barnsley districts.

# *The Cutting Edge*

In these cynical spin-doctored days it is easy to forget just how heartfelt was the belief in socialism in the first part of the twentieth century. Before the first world war when the Labour party was still in nappies and communism was still a respected, if untested, political and economic doctrine feelings ran high amongst the politically aware. Long before the fall of the Berlin wall, before the rise and fall of the Soviet Union, before Stalin, Chairman Mao and Fidel Castro it is all too easy to forget that many people believed with an almost religious intensity that it really was possible to build a Workers' Paradise if only...

The story of Sheffield's Swann-Morton Company, now an internationally famous firm manufacturing more than a million surgical and craft blades every single day, is a unique tale of selfless devotion to a work force and the practical application of political principles which are almost unheard of today.

> ## *Mr Swann's founding principles*
>
> *1. Claims of individuals producing in an industry came first, before anything else, and must always remain first. They are the human beings on which everything is built.*
>
> *2. If the industry cannot pay the rightful reward of labour (while they are producing profit for the owners) then a new policy is required on the part of the management to make it do so.*
>
> *3. If the management can't do the job, then a new management is required, as well as a new policy.*
>
> *4. Individuals in any industry have a perfect right to demand and see that this objective is reached, <u>because they produce the goods</u>.*

In August 1932, with a capital of just £150, the firm started to make and sell a range of razor blades. Nothing but razor blades was seriously considered at the time although the company papers show that cutlery knives, scissors and agricultural instruments were amongst the ideas in the founders' minds.

True to their philosophy, even before they began business, the founders drew up four statements to guide them in the social consequences of their entry into the capitalist world. These four statements were written out on the firm's headed note paper in Walter R Swann's handwriting, one copy of which has survived the ensuing years.

***Above:*** *The founders' four statements, written to guide them on their entry into the capitalist world.*
***Below:*** *Swann Morton's first premises in 1932.*

It was in 1917, the year of the Russian revolution, that after leaving grammar school Walter Swann became an apprentice engineer. From that time to 1924 his experiences turned him into a revolutionary socialist. In 1924 he found himself working as craftsman fitter with a Miss Doris Fairweather who was a supervisor in charge of a group of women making razor blades on grinding machines.

In 1925 Swann was offered a position to establish a razor blade department in another firm; he accepted not only because he wanted more responsibility but also because he was close to being sacked for his trade union and agitating activities.

Doris Fairweather together with a number of women in her charge and another fitter joined Swann in working for the new firm.

Six years later the team was disillusioned. It had become evident that if one could not look after oneself nobody else would. In 1932 W R Swann & Co Ltd was founded. The founding team was made up of Walter R Swann, a metallurgist J Alfred Morton, Doris Fairweather, a fitter and the team of women whom Doris supervised.

The new business began in a workshop behind houses in Sheffield's Woodlands Street. Miss Fairweather, as she was always known, was a strong disciplinarian, a trait no doubt inherited from her father who had been a regimental sergeant major. The hopeful band nearly came unstuck but by the end of one year a very, very small firm was in being.

They built their own machinery, developed new devices as simple as possible, kept quality and service at a very high level and put all profits back into growth; with good administration and inspection by 1935 they were soundly based and made a move to marginally better premises in Bradfield Road.

**Above:** *The second factory founded in 1935 on Bradfield Road, Sheffield* **Below:** *Company founders Miss Doris Fairweather and Mr W R Swann.*

It was about this time, the firm's name having become noted for good quality in fine edges, that it was approached by a surgical house to make replaceable blades for scalpels with a patented design of handle. Never having seen anything like this before they went into the matter feeling that another string to their bow would make for further stability and consolidation. The sales for that type of handle however did not come up to expectations and the work came to an end. They had though discovered that the American firm Bard Parker was the originator of this type of article and that its patent had run out. So it was decided not to allow Swann-Morton's research and new know-how to be wasted. Accordingly the firm made tools and the Swann-Morton scalpel was born. In the long run they were fully justified in the effort put into this work: today they can boast 90 per cent of the British trade in such products with exports to over 100 countries.

From 1935 until the outbreak of war in 1939 there was rapid growth, it was a very exciting time in all ways. At Christmas time substantial cash presents were given to all workers; in those days an unusual and very much appreciated gesture.

In keeping with the principle of caring for workers a 40 hour working week was started, an innovation which was soon followed with greater publicity by Boots of Nottingham. All holidays were paid for by the company, more workers were recruited, money

**Right:** *Grinding razor blades in the early years.*
**Above right:** *Some of the firm's staff in April 1944.*
**Top:** *The growing factory in 1939.*

was saved and by 1938 the firm bought the first piece of land for the erection of part of the present factory, the Penn works at Owlerton Green. The first four workshops were completed in 1939 just as the war started. Surgical knives were required in

ever greater quantities and as the company's technical efficiency increased it was able to reduce prices, which it did, the directors having no desire to make profit out of the country's troubles and be seen as war profiteers. That policy turned out to be a mistake as customers thought that the quality couldn't be good at such a low price.

The same sort of response had been seen in earlier years with razor blades of which the firm sold more when it increased the price. Such lessons, and many others about human behaviour, were eventually well learned. With a cruel irony, given the firm's founding principles, the application of socialism caused it great problems after the war. With the Labour government elected at the war's end taxation was increased to ominous proportions. Even so the company still went forward with its growth policy and the second stage of building took place at Owlerton Green producing the administration and office block as well as flats for Walter Swann and a caretaker. By that time the firm had a work force of approximately 100.

Alfred Morton left the company in the post war period leaving Walter Swann and Doris Fairweather as remaining co-directors.

With possible unemployment in Scotland the pair thought they would do well to start a factory there for razor blade making. This again was a mistake; an example of sentimentality overriding commercial judgement.

After seven months working they closed down the Scottish factory and pruned Sheffield, getting down to a period of austere working to pay their taxes. Politics, economics, finance. They knew something about the first two but nothing about the third. They learned the hard way and eventually came up smiling. Before then however Purchase Tax had been applied to razor blades and the last straw came when the firm had to pay tax on one million razor blades given away free as samples in a selling campaign.

During the fifties the company decided to steadily run down the making of razor blades having had enough taxation and set about concentrating on scalpels and fine industrial edges on which there was no tax.

It was in 1957 that a superannuation scheme was started, at first limited to the key people within the organisation. This was of great benefit. Two directors and a secretary had died as well as others including the first fitter who had been with the firm from the outset; the result being their widows were reasonably well provided for.

*Left: Designers in the Drawing Office.* **Below:** *The works canteen in the 1940s. Mr Swann leaning and Miss Fairweather, right.*

The directors still felt that a strong organisation should be used to look after individuals in adversity and this they did.

During the ten years from 1947 to 1957, despite their tax troubles, the firm went on with its third stage of building putting everything back into plant and buildings with the exception of the few thousand pounds paid out to workers at Christmas time.

The volume of production was growing, technical efficiency and research improving all the time producing ever increasing profits. By 1957 the firm was manufacturing 38 million blades each year, 100,000 each working day and using 140 tons of Sheffield-made strip steel.

In an unexpected sideways move Walter Swann decided to invest in food production creating a profitable orchard which could cheaply supply at least part of the workforce's food needs. By 1961 S M (Growers) came into being with orchard land and properties in the Wisbech area of Cambridge. Packing buildings and cold storage chambers were built to the same high standard that characterised the Sheffield factory. Many thousands of young trees were planted and everything was done to lay the foundations for modern fruit growing in a competitive world.

At Sheffield by 1964 the fourth stage of building took place giving still more productive capacity. Shortly after that building the demand for sterilised surgical blades began to increase. As the firm had been the prime movers in the use of Vapour Phase Inhibitor - VPI - paper inserted into foil to keep blades clean and dry and non-rusting, they got in touch with UKAE at Wantage and with its co-operation developed the sterilisation of blades through gamma radiation.

**Top left:** *Surgical blade packaging in the mid 1960s.*
**Above right:** *The busy handle department.*
**Right:** *An exhibition stand at the British Industries Fair, Olympia in 1945.*

After a while it became clear that a cobalt plant on the premises would soon become a necessity as a part of the production line, so in late 1964 a batch cobalt plant, the first of its kind in the world, was erected in new premises built for that purpose. Visitors from many countries visited the works solely to see the new plant. Soon after being installed the throughput was such that further cobalt had to be loaded to cut down the sterilisation time in order to keep pace with growing production and orders.

A dedicated core of people spent their working lifetimes in creating wealth and welding together a team of ordinary people to achieve a dream. In keeping with their socialist principles the directors felt that whilst an imaginative technical and administrative

and commercial staff were essential to keep up the good works they neither needed nor wanted other shareholders outside of those who worked in the business. Indeed until the trustees' company was formed no dividends were ever paid.

As the wealth had been created, first out of the shaving public, then out of sick people throughout the world, the directors continued to believe that the wealth created should not be turned into currency for a few people to consume but to be used first in the interests of those who made it and then in the surgical and medical world.

In the mid 1960s Mr Swann was mindful of the future security of the company, his workforce and the founding principles, upon which everything was based. A trust was formed to administer the company within which the employees had a 50 per cent share, the remaining 50 per cent in a charitable holding. Sadly, Mr Swann died in October 1980 and his co-director, Doris Fairweather died in February 1984 but their foresight in the 1960s ensured that this unique arrangement has seen the company go from strength to strength.

Achieving today's quality standards and complying with multifarious rules and regulations may prove difficult for some companies, but for Swann-Morton it has just been a natural progression.

Operating a policy of self design and build wherever possible gives the company a high degree of control over its production processes - and ideas for improvement from the factory floor are positively encouraged. Management has never held back from the introduction of new technology and this has consistently put the company at the leading edge of surgical blade manufacture.

The installation of its own irradiation plant in the 1960s gave Swann-Morton complete self-sufficiency in product sterilisation and since the introduction in the late eighties of a state of the art irradiation centre complete with micro-biological laboratory it is able to offer these facilities to other healthcare manufacturers.

*Above:* The factory taking shape in the 1950s.
*Below:* Heat treatment in the 1980s.

Quality control has always been of utmost importance at Swann-Morton with inspections taking place throughout the production processes. Indeed surgical blades are subject to two final inspections immediately prior to packaging the blade within a 'clean room' environment, after which blades are sterilised in the on-site gamma irradiation facility, a service performed by the subsidiary company Swann-Morton (Services) Ltd. Such separation ensures total independence and control over all processes and subject to available capacity is a service which is offered under contract to outside organisations.

To complete the comprehensive facilities an in-house microbiological laboratory provides an expert service for monitoring and identifying microbiol contamination both environmental and product-borne ensuring the highest possible standards for Swann-Morton products' sterility levels.

At the turn of the new century Swann-Morton has marked its progress and achievements by embarking on an extensive expansion programme involving major construction works to increase Despatch and sterile Storage facilities, Workshop and production areas, new Laboratories and new Administration accommodation. That substantial investment of five and a half million pounds underlines Swann-Morton's commitment to, and confidence in, the future.

The company's focus not only on product quality but also on quality of service maintains continuing high standards throughout the supply chain within both the domestic and overseas markets. Whilst new opportunities within the Capitalist West still

present themselves to the company, especially in the USA, Swann-Morton still invests time and expertise in developing the markets which are still emerging from years of communist rule and again appears to be laying firm foundations for the future growth of its business.

Today the company employs around 280 people and uses 500 tonnes of steel each year to make around 1.25 million surgical and craft blades each day which are sold in virtually every country in the world. Almost two thirds of production is exported with a turnover exceeding £13 million a year.

***Above:*** *Walter's - the firm's new cafeteria.*
***Top:*** *The increasingly hi-tech world of the Furnace Shop in 2000.*

Swann-Morton blades are used in the most demanding environment of all - the operating theatre. For use there, continual development in response to customer demand has led to the creation of over sixty surgical blades and more than twenty handles. As surgical techniques have become ever more sophisticated Swann-Morton has risen to the challenges posed by modern surgical techniques.

But the company's surgical blades are not only used in operating theatres; the are also the choice of dentists, chiropodists and veterinary surgeons and a host of professionals in industry, crafts and art studios. Wherever a truly versatile, precision cutting blade is needed on every continent one will find a Swann-Morton product close at hand.

The same principles which led to Swann-Morton's founding still apply. The firm still has an extraordinary low turnover of employees who enjoy unique working conditions that include ten weeks holiday a year, a thirty-five hour week, double time for overtime, profit related pay, private health care and a contributory pension scheme. There can be few businesses that have been founded on a Utopian dream that have lasted beyond the lifetime of their

*Above:* Part of the major expansion to the Packing Department. *Below:* The new Reception area.

founders, or which have continued to follow their original values despite becoming a major undertaking.

The legacy of Walter Swann and Doris Fairweather provides an extraordinary testimonial to their socialist values - and a continuing example to others of what can be achieved through applying genuine moral principles in an otherwise harsh and cynical world.

The elements which combine to make Swann-Morton the triumph it is today will carry it forward into the 21st century with confidence and purpose. The desire for ongoing improvement, the hard work ethic of all its employees and a policy of promotion from within will sustain it as a world leader and undoubtedly take Swann-Morton to even greater heights to the benefit of the company, its employees and their customers.

And is Swann-Morton a workers paradise? Perhaps it is true that perfection will never be attained on Earth. Marxism, Communism and any other number of fashionable isms alongside Anarchy and Hippiedom have come and gone down the years. And yet Swan-Morton has survived them all. An idea put into action will only flourish if the original idea was a sound one. The continuing existence of Swann-Morton confounds all what those pundits would have us believe about human nature.

# Tools for the Record Book

One of the most familiar names in Sheffield is Record Tools, part of the Record Ridgway Group based at the Parkway Works.

The Record Ridgway Group was formed in September 1972 by the merger of two long-established companies in the hand tool industry: C & J Hampton Ltd and William Ridgway & Sons Ltd. As each company at that date also had a 50 per cent holding in an even older company, William Marples & Sons Ltd, that too became an integral part of the group. Each of the three firms had a long history behind it.

### C & J Hampton Ltd.

In 1898 two brothers Charles and Joseph Hampton left the family business the Steel Nut and Joseph Hampton Limited in Wednesbury, Staffordshire to come to Sheffield to set up their own business in Attercliffe. Their partnership was called 'C & J Hampton' and its range of ferrous products included tools, jacks, marine shackles and flywheel castings. Shortly afterwards the brothers fell out and Joseph Hampton returned to Wednesbury. Soon after the turn of the century

Charles' two sons Horace and Charles W Hampton joined their father in the business.

After ten years sales had reached £6,000 pa and on 14th May 1908 a private limited company C & J Hampton Limited was incorporated with an authorised capital of £10,000. The following year the decision was taken to concentrate on the manufacture of hand tools and the 'RECORD' trade mark was registered for the first time in the UK and certain overseas countries. During the 1920s and 1930s the product range was expanded to include pipe tools, planes, bolt cutters and vices. A sales network was established which gradually extended into overseas markets and the company's products under the Record name became brand leaders with an enviable reputation for quality and durability. In 1929 Charles Hampton died and his two sons became joint managing directors.

**Above:** *William Ridgway.*
**Below:** *Staff from Marples wooden plane department pictured in 1920.*

name changed to Record Tools (Pty) Limited. In the same year Charles W Hampton died and Tony Hampton succeeded him as Chairman. In 1959 some of the assets of M C Gooding & Co Limited, a small tool manufacturing company in London trading as Keen Tools, was purchased and its operation moved to Sheffield; products included a range of low-priced hand drills and hand bench grinders. A new company called Fabrex Tools Ltd was formed to market these under the Fabrex name as a springboard into the DIY market, supplemented by a range of light-duty vices. However it was found to be extremely difficult both to manufacture and to sell side by side two product ranges of differing quality standards and the Fabrex range was discontinued nine years later.

In 1936 the company acquired premises at Bernard Road which were to remain the Head Office until the move to the present Parkway Works. Profits rose from £1,000 in 1915 to £10,000 in 1926 and £100,000 in 1942. In 1946 the Record Tool Company Limited was formed to protect the brand name.

In 1948 Horace Hampton died and the company went public with an issued capital of £100,000. In the same year Charles W Hampton became Chairman and his son Tony Hampton joined the Board. By 1952 profit exceeded £200,000 on sales of £1.25 million and a Canadian company, another Record Tools Limited, was set up in Montreal to provide a warehousing operation in North America. In 1954 a new factory was built at Kettelbridge on the edge of what is now known as the Parkway site for the production of components many of which were previously bought in.

In 1958 the Fabricated Tool Company in Benoni South Africa (trade mark 'FABREX' ) was purchased and the

In 1961 Woden Tools Limited was purchased from the Steel Nut & Joseph Hampton company in Wednesbury and its products integrated into the Record range, the Woden trademark continuing to be used for some ten years. In 1963 William Marples & Sons Limited was acquired jointly with William Ridgway & Sons Limited; in that same year the company moved to new offices and factory premises at Parkway which formed the nucleus of the present Parkway Works.

The Bestmore Tool & Edge Tool Co. Limited of Hednesford, Staffordshire was acquired in 1971; this company manufactured a wide range of hammers under various brand names and also sold forgings to the trade; the acquisition presented the opportunity to add a Record hammer to the range.

***Above left:*** *William Ridgway's Edward Street premises.* ***Top:*** *Auger twisting at Edward Street.*

By 1972 the Hampton Group comprised eight companies with a total annual turnover of £4.3 million and had 930 employees in the UK.

### William Ridgway & Sons Limited

In 1898 William Ridgway was working as a skilled hand forger of augers and auger bits. Trade was not good but he decided to set up his own business, borrowing five pounds to supplement his own five pounds savings. By improving the design of the wood boring tools then in use his business prospered.

In 1900 William moved to larger premises and was joined by two of his sons, Oscar and Jack. On 16th July 1909 a private limited company William Ridgway & Sons Limited was incorporated with an authorised capital of £500. William Ridgway's third son, Stanley, later also joined the firm. In 1920 Jack Ridgway became managing director and in 1926 Donald Ridgway , Oscar's son, joined the company; and in 1927 Bob Phillips, another grandson of William Ridgway, also came into the family business.

In 1936 William Ridgway died. At about the same time a machine tool (MT) division was formed to manufacture router cutters and wood boring tools for use in wood-working machines complementing the hand tool range. Ridgways developed into the largest specialist manufacturer of wood boring tools in the world. A brand new factory at Meadow Street together with an office and warehouse block was built in stages between 1952 and 1958. Around that time the company sought to consolidate its position within the specialist woodworking tool field by acquiring other companies. In 1956 Alexander Mathieson & Sons Limited was acquired: established in Glasgow in 1792 this was once a very large tool manufacturing company which at the time of Queen Victoria's death had 1,000 employees and a turnover in excess of £1 million. In 1957 Charles Neil & Co Limited was acquired; this company manufactured woodboring tools for machine use and router cutters complementary to the Ridgway range.

In 1962 Jack Ridgway died and Ridgways acquired another company which had been owned by him: W A Timperley Limited. Two years later the company went public.

***Above:*** *An exhibition stand at the British Empire Exhibition in 1925.* ***Top:*** *The Packing Department at Ridgway's Edward Street premises in 1920.*

The Gilbow Tool & Steel Co Limited, well known for its range of tinsnips and cold chisels, was purchased in 1966.

In the same year a 51 per cent interest was acquired in an Australian company, Tool Engineering & Service Company Proprietary Limited and its name changed to Ridgway-Tesco Pty Limited. That company, located in Melbourne, was mainly concerned with the manufacture of woodworking cutter equipment and, along with its subsidiary Tescutters Limited in Sydney, the import into Australia of woodworking machinery. It was decided that this venture would form a useful association with the Ridgway MT division and would also be used as a possible base for the future manufacture in Australia of the Ridgway range. Finally in 1968 Clico (Sheffield) Limited was acquired; this company was a customer of Ridgway's MT division and supplied both wood and metal working tools to a wide range of outlets including the aircraft and furniture industries.

By 1972 the Ridgway Group comprised nine companies with a total annual turnover of £1.5 million and had around 500 employees in the UK.

### *William Marples & Sons Limited*

William Marples learned his trade in his father's business as a joiner's tool and skate manufacturers. In 1828 at the age of 21 he set up in business on his own and by 1859 he was doing so well that he had to move to larger premises at Westfield Terrace where his three sons Edwin Henry, William Kent and Albert joined him. In 1869 the founder retired leaving his sons to run the company. In 1871 another local firm, Turner & Naylor, was acquired and by 1888 the two younger sons had retired leaving Edwin Henry, the eldest, as sole proprietor.

In 1898 the firm became a private limited company, William Marples & Sons Limited, and Edwin Henry Marples was joined on the board by his two elder sons Henry Edgar and Edward Albert and later by the youngest, John Kent. In 1908 Edwin Henry retired leaving John Kent in charge. In 1912 Geoffrey Marples a son of Henry Edgar joined the company and in 1923 Alan O'Connor Fenton, great grandson of the founder entered the family business. Over the years the factory at Westfield Terrace was gradually extended by the purchase of adjoining premises. After the second world war Peter Marples (John Kent's son) and Jim Marples (son of Geoffrey) also joined the company on their release from the Royal Air Force.

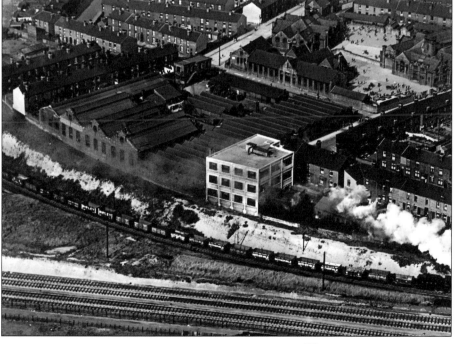

*Above right: An advert for Marples' Hibernia Works **Above left:** The Ouse Road Foundry in 1950. **Left:** Ouse Road pictured in 1932.*

In 1963 when the company was acquired jointly by C & J Hampton Limited and William Ridgway & Sons Limited it became apparent that the premises at Westfield Terrace were not conducive to efficient manufacture. A site had already been acquired at Dronfield in the late 1950s and a small woodturning factory built there; this was extended and the old premises were finally vacated in 1970.

By 1972 Marples had an annual turnover of around £1.25 million and over 200 employees.

### The Record Ridgway Group

When C & J Hampton and William Ridgway & Sons merged on 29 September 1972 the result was a tool group made up of no less than fourteen UK companies plus five overseas employing between them some 1,700 people. Premises were scattered all over Sheffield as well as those at Hednesford and abroad. The product range was enormous though fortunately with few overlaps. Tony Hampton became chairman of the new Group and Bob Phillips was appointed Deputy Chairman.

C & J Hampton Limited was renamed Record Ridgway Limited and became the parent company of the new

group, all other companies becoming direct subsidiaries. William Ridgway & Sons Limited was renamed Record Ridgway Tools Limited and became the principal operating company taking over the assets of all the other Sheffield companies with the sole exception of Clico (Sheffield) Limited which was retained as a separate 'independent' outlet. All the other Sheffield companies became dormant and two were 'sacrificed' and their names changed to preserve the original Hampton and Ridgway company titles.

A programme of rationalisation was started, covering product range, manufacturing operations, premises and management. Group turnover in 1973 was over £7.5 million, some 45 per cent of which was sold overseas.

*Top:* Wm. Ridgway workers at Rockingham Street, taken in 1914. *Above:* The Wood Vice department on Ouse Road. *Left:* An aerial view of Marples' factory on Meadow Street.

machines, bandsaws and woodworking machinery accessories. A series of acquisitions also followed in the mid nineties including Bulldog Tools in Wigan, makers of contractors, agricultural and gardening tools; Startrite Machines in Rochester making industrial saws and Hilmor Ltd, famous for their pipe bending tools and equipment.

In 1998 the Board decided to accept an offer from American Tool Companies Inc. American Tool is the largest, privately owned international tool manufacturer employing 4200 people in 23 manufacturing plants around the world and has a long tradition of producing and selling premier quality hand tools to both professional and amateur craftsmen under such famous brands as; Vise-Grip® locking tools, Quick-Grip® clamps, Irwin® power tool accessories and Jack® handsaws. In short, Record and its new owners share the same philosophy of making quality products marketed under reputable brand names.

American Tool Companies worldwide sales and marketing organisation has opened up a wealth of new markets to Sheffield made Record products. In addition, Record is now able to expand its market share by promoting and selling the wide range of hand tools and power tool accessories produced by American Tool companies.

At the start of the new millennium, the future for Record tools never looked brighter.

How many thousands of Sheffield men over the years must have worked for one or other of the companies which eventually came to make up the Record Group and how extraordinary to realise just how complex the evolution of such businesses can seem when viewed over a period of a century or more. Looking at the past who would dare guess what further changes the future might bring?

***Above:*** *Some of the modern day products produced in Record's Sheffield factories.*
***Below:*** *Record's Parkway headquarters today.*

Demand for the new Group's products escalated and delivery times soon became very extended. Part of the problem was due to difficulties in obtaining reliable supplies of malleable castings and forgings; the malleable casting problem was alleviated by the construction of a foundry in 1973 and it was decided to purchase a forging company to solve the other half of the problem. Platt Forgings Limited of Willenhall, Staffordshire, was acquired in 1976 and the modernisation of that company's plant was included in a £5 million capital development programme, the other main component of which was the construction of a new grey iron foundry on the Parkway site to replace the existing foundry in Ouse Road.

In 1977 Record Ridgway won the Queen's Award for Export Achievement but in 1978 overseas demand abruptly declined. In the face of escalating costs the work force was reduced by redundancies and again in 1979. Group turnover was maintained during 1980 at around £20 million as a result of regular price increases but the recession in the UK was beginning to bite and profit margins were falling rapidly.

The new foundry became operational during 1980 and due partly to the start up costs the Group made a loss that year. The decision was made to dispose of Platts Forgings in view of its increasing losses and it was finally sold in early 1981 when Bestmore Tools Limited was also closed due to lack of orders.

During 1980 discussions started with AB Bahco of Sweden on the possibility of manufacturing certain Bahco products in Sheffield; those talks culminated in Bahco making a bid for Record Ridgway which was finally accepted on 27 February 1981.

Toward the end of 1985 a management buy out returned the Company to British ownership and in the last quarter of 1987 Record Holdings plc was listed on the Stock Market. This flotation provided Record with much needed capital with which it developed the very successful Sheffield based Record Power Tool division, manufacturing woodturning lathes, drilling and morticing

# *Investing in Sheffield*

Money is never far from a Yorkshireman's thoughts. With offices in Sheffield one of Britain's most prominent investment companies is BWD Rensburg. The history of the firm has many strands, one of the most important leading back to the origins of the Sheffield Stock Exchange.

The Sheffield Stock Exchange came into existence on 4th October 1844. One of its earliest meeting places was at 2 Church Street but in 1873 the Exchange had moved to rooms above a shop in the High Street.

Further accommodation was rented from time to time until the former Head Post Office premises in Haymarket and Commercial Street were purchased and converted into the Stock Exchange Building which opened on 6th November 1911.

The importance of the Exchange grew along with the development of the iron and steel industry in the district, whilst its location at the geographical centre of the most important coalfields in the country gave the Sheffield Exchange an enhanced status and it quickly became the recognised market for colliery shares in the region.

By the late 60s the Sheffield Stock Exchange was located in York Street having become the Northern Stock Exchange (Sheffield Unit)in 1967. Six years later, in 1973, it was abolished after federation with the London Stock Exchange.

Back in 1875 however the Sheffield Exchange boasted 27 members amongst whom were included Jarvis and Christopher Barber trading as Barber Brothers & Wortley of Alliance Chambers in George Street, Joseph Becket Wostinholm of 10 Norfolk Row, Henry Hart of Hart & Moss in Rotherham, Marriott Oakes of Norfolk Row, and

**Right:** *A painting of early 19th century East Parade, Sheffield.*

Charles and Francis Smith of George Street, all names which would feature in Sheffield's stockbroking history for many decades to follow.

The Sheffield firm of Nicholson Barber came about as a result of a merger in 1981 between Christopher Barber & Wostinholm and JW Nicholson & Sons. The choice of Barber Nicholson or Nicholson Barber being decided amicably by spinning a coin. In February 1988 one of BWDR's precursors, Battye Wimpenny and Dawson of Huddersfield acquired Walter Ward & Co, which started trading in Campo Lane in 1923 and which itself had absorbed Oakes Belk & Skinner in 1974.

To the outsider the history of mergers, amalgamations and acquisitions over tens of decades can sometimes seem like a cat's cradle of changing names, but within that tangled skein are many fascinating threads. It is perhaps the family names Nicholson and Barber

which will be longest associated with the history of stockbroking in Sheffield. The Barber brothers, Jarvis and Christopher, had been members of the Sheffield Exchange since 1867 and 1870 respectively. Their father James had featured in White's Directory of Sheffield as early as 1857.

The Barber family owed its good fortune to a theft. Whilst working as a junior clerk at a bank James Barber discovered that one of the bank's staff had stolen deeds and securities from the safe and taken ship to the USA. Acting on his own initiative James had immediately taken a ticket on a faster ship and met the errant individual when his slower vessel docked. By strength of character, or perhaps muscle, James retrieved his employers' assets and on his return to

*Above: East Parade in 1900.* **Top:** *Commercial Street in 1893.*

England was royally rewarded with sufficient funds to subsequently enable him to set up his sons in business.

The history of stockbroking and investment in Sheffield is however perhaps best illustrated by the story of the Nicholson family.

Sometime before 1860 one James Nicholson had moved to Sheffield from Banbury starting up as a 'little mester' in the cutlery trade, describing himself as a spring knife cutler - an outworker with very low overheads and perhaps employing up to ten men and boys using rented grinding troughs.

James Willis Nicholson, 'JWN' as he later became known, was born in 1860. At the age of twelve he left school to help his father for a wage of one shilling a week. He soon realised that to get on in the world he would have to do something different and went to work for Hunt & Gill estate agents in Norfolk Row as an office boy. He was a good writer and after teaching himself shorthand became a junior clerk before transferring to the firm of stockbrokers FE & S Smith.

JWN aimed to be chairman of the Sheffield Stock Exchange, which he eventually became in 1907. But before then there was much to achieve. Having gone to work for the FE & S Smith in the early 1880s he became partner in 1899 and remained there until 1909 when the firm was dissolved and he decided to start up in business on his own from premises at 5 East Parade. The firm of JW Nicholson & Son came into being when his eldest son, Cyril, became a partner in 1912. Cyril the eldest of JWN's six sons had been born in 1887 and during an active life made and lost at least

three fortunes; his Managing Clerk used to say that 'if Mr Cyril were to fall from the top of Chesterfield Church he would drop into a new suit'. He certainly had a flair for making money, though seemingly rather less ability to keep it.

In 1934 Cyril Nicholson bought Firbeck Hall and the Parkhill estate of 2,500 acres; he converted the Hall into a country club providing a first class 18 hole golf course. Two years later Cyril also bought Sheffield's Grand Hotel, from the receiver and subsequently almost rebuilt it with a new entrance and underground garage.

Returning however to the 19th century, in 1857 the Directory of the Borough of Sheffield contains the name of Ebenezer Smith & Son amongst the fifteen firms of Sheffield stock and share brokers most of whom also practised as accountants and estate agents. The Sheffield Stock Exchange being inaugurated in 1844 and Ebenezer Smith was elected a member two years later and his son, Francis Ebenezer 'FE' Smith in 1848.

FE's brother Sydney became a Stock Exchange member in 1857 and the name of the firm changed to FE & S Smith, a name retained for half a century. FE Smith lived in great style at Botanical Villa and later at Whirlow Grange. In later years FE drove daily to his

office in his carriage picking up his young partner JW Nicholson at the bottom of Bents Road, since in those days the horse trams went only as far as Hunters Bar. Sadly FE died almost penniless in 1906.

JW Nicholson had become a partner in 1899 the year he became a member of the Stock

***Top:*** *Commercial Street in 1905.* ***Above right:*** *The new electronic dealing board, built by Ericcsons, in the new offices at Telephone Buildings.* ***Right:*** *The dealing board seen from behind.*

Exchange. On the death of FE Smith and the retirement of Sydney Smith he was joined in partnership by the, unrelated, David Thurston Smith. The profits of the firm for the three years 1906-09 averaged £3,000 per annum, a large sum for the times, even when divided by two. There was however unhappiness in the firm and two clerks JH Holmes and JW Judge persuaded David Smith to dissolve the partnership and form the new firm of Smith, Holmes and Judge followed by a third clerk Herbert Coates who much later became the sole partner in that venture.

On the dissolution of the old firm JWN founded his own business, starting up in August 1909 in offices consisting of just two rooms - a private office and a general office. He appears to have retained many of

his old clients, profits for the first three years averaging £1,500.

In 1912 when JWN's son Cyril was taken into partnership the firm's name changed to JW Nicholson & Son and by 1919 it employed a staff of eight.

Commissions gradually grew and by the close of war in 1918 Cyril's one eighth share of the business' annual profits alone came to £500. Not every year led to profit however, and a severe slump in the early 1920s led to three years of losses being recorded.

Despite the vagaries of business a move had been made in the Autumn of 1919 to 2 High Street above the offices of the Union Bank of Manchester (later Barclays Bank). A separate dealing room was established to cope with the operation of extensive private telephone lines and teleprinters. Country jobbing, a market-making service to stockbrokers countrywide provided by JWNS, started to take off.

By 1927 the firm's trading volume exceeded an astonishing fifteen million pounds a year and the number of staff had increased to fifty. Three members of the family were admitted to membership of the Sheffield Stock Exchange: JWN's sons Arnold and Philip and his son-in-law Frank Booker. The name of the firm became J W Nicholson & Sons in 1927 and soon became a legend.

***Left and below:*** *A busy exchange in the 1930s.*

In 1932 the firm's founder JWN had died after spending over fifty years in stockbroking and his son Cyril became the senior partner.

The firm had moved into new offices at Telephone Buildings where a new dealing room was established on the ground floor; at first prices were marked up on a black board but that was soon superseded by an electronically operated board specially built by Ericssons in 1933. By that time the firm was sending out a thousand mail shots each day to the provincial brokers who used Nicholsons' services.

The thirties was a decade of change; office equipment had originally been designed to cope with five hundred bargains daily; book keeping machines were superseded in 1935 by a battery of copying machines which were themselves superseded only three years later by a complete punched card installation which helped increase output to over two and a half thousand transactions every day - ten per cent of all share transactions in the UK!

The heart of the business at Telephone Buildings was an air conditioned dealing room with a separate teleprinter room operating in over two hundred active stocks all controlled by the partners with four principal dealers, four assistant dealers and 32 telephone operators dealing through a network of private telephone and teleprinter lines. The firm was reputed to be the second largest subscriber in the country to the telephone exchange with its 15 exchange lines and even a teleprinter line to New York.

By 1936 almost two hundred staff were being employed and annual profits were averaging six figures.

The popularity of country jobbing and the service provided by J W Nicholson & Sons had not gone unnoticed by the London Stock Exchange so new rules were introduced in 1941 outlawing dealings by members with 'non-member jobbers' inevitably declaring J W Nicholson & Sons non-member jobbers.

Consequently, the firm decided to split and Cyril Nicholson continued jobbing under considerable restriction, finally giving up in the early fifties to develop other interests in the South. The 'clients' side of the business had not been developed for upwards of twenty years and the name of J W Nicholson & Sons was transferred to the stockbroking firm and a rapid

**Both pictures:** *Two of the offices in Telephone Buildings in the mid 1930s, in styles very typical of the time.*

build up of private client business followed the end of the War. For the next forty years Nicholsons and Barbers dominated the local scene, particularly after their amalgamation in 1981. The name was eponymous with stockbroking in Sheffield.

For a variety of reasons the number of local companies quoted on the London Stock Exchange has contracted considerably over the past 25 years and dealing in them by local firms, followed the trend. However, prior to Federation in 1973, dealings in local companies provided a significant proportion of the business of the Sheffield stockbrokers. Both Barbers and Nicholsons also had some 'new issue' business. This aspect of the business had enabled the development of close ties with London Institutions on the one hand and local industry on the other. It also enhanced the private client business due to the close-knit nature of the Sheffield business and investment community - Sheffield is often referred to as the 'largest village in England'. In fact, the loyalties and close relationships existing between the investing public and the local stockbroking community, contributed to the survival of firms during the very difficult conditions of the protracted 1974 'Bear Market'. For many years post Federation, Tony West, a partner of Barbers and in due course Senior Partner of Nicholson-Barber, served with distinction on the Council of the Stock Exchange.

In October 1999 when the firm of BWD Rensburg became the successor to the renowned Sheffield business of Nicholson Barber the two firms both had an impressive past. Henry Edward Rensburg was born in the Dutch port of The Hague in 1841 but went to Liverpool in 1863 at the age of 22 to join the staff of bankers Edward Yates and Company, eventually becoming a board member of that firm.

In 1873 Rensburg was elected as a member of the London Stock Exchange with a capital fund of £10,000. Rensburg's primary business at that time was shunting stocks and shares - balancing supply and demand between the London Stock Exchange and provincial exchanges such as those in Liverpool, Manchester and Sheffield. The 'BWD' part of the present name was already in existence at that time as an abbreviation of Battye, Wimpenny and Dawson

a Huddersfield firm which would not merge with the Rensburg business for another century.

During the 1960s and 70s many mergers took place. In 1969 the acquisition of the firm of Middleton, Hanby and Kimber of Bradford established Rensburg's first Yorkshire base. BWD Rensberg, the major subsidiary of BWD Securities, was established in 1989 on the merger with Battye, Wimpenny and Dawson.

The company now manages funds for clients totalling more than two and a half billion pounds. In addition to advising on stocks and shares BWD Rensburg has financial planning teams which can give financial advice on a wide range of financial topics such as retirement planning, inheritance tax and tax-efficient investment.

In addition to looking after private individuals the firm has a growing charity and pension fund and unit trust management teams. The firm has a proven investment record demonstrated by a succession of performance awards.

Today BWD Rensburg Investment Management operates from eight offices in Liverpool, Leeds, Manchester, Doncaster, Chesterfield, Belfast, Glasgow and of course Sheffield where the city's stockbrokers have always aimed to provide a quality personal service, combining a national outlook with local accessibility.

**Left:** *Dealing Room, Sheffield Unit Northern Stock Exchange, York Street circa 1971. Most of the members mark the retirement of Leslie Brown, Secretary.*
**Below:** *Most of the members outside Sheffield Cathedral to mark the passing of the Sheffield Stock Exchange (Northern Unit) prior to Federation in 1973.*

# A hundred years of haulage

**M**ention Loxley to most people and Robin Hood springs to mind. But, to the Askey family, Loxley means the original site of their business. Over a century ago, the first of four generations of Askeys carried on their haulage trade from Glass Tilt House in Loxley Bottoms. To this day, apart from when the company moved to Middlewood Road in 1959, the firm has remained on the banks of the River Loxley at various sites along its length. To say that the family lived and worked the business is very true. This was the family home as well as the base from which the horses and carts began plying their trade.

These were the days when Victoria was on the throne. Horse power meant just what it said. Powerful beasts pulled carts laden with heavy loads along the cobbled streets, their shoes sparking on the stones as they clip-clopped along the way. On high days and holidays these magnificent creatures would be decked out in gleaming harnesses and highly polished brasses. Plumed headdresses swayed in the breeze as the drivers proudly showed off their charges. There was always time for special parades and celebrations to show that people could take a pride in their work and its appearance. Although the horses were basically tools of the trade, the Askeys recognised that they were God's creatures as well. It was both Christian and practical to make sure that they were well fed and cared for. It was part of the Victorian set of values that you worked hard, but also acknowledged that you were part of a larger spiritual world. The stables and mill at Glass Tilt House are still in existence today. They stand as a monument to those far off days when the firm we now know as Askey Transport was starting out on the long road to success.

Family businesses were part and parcel of everyday life. This family was no exception. Originally owned by John Wood it was taken over in 1902 by Willis and Charlotte Askey (nee Wood) from

*Above left: Harold Askey.* **Right:** *The bill of sale for the company dated November 2nd 1902.* **Below:** *Three horses in tandem outside Glass Tilt House.*

was a limit on the weight that they could pull and new 20th century technology would gradually see their demise. It was the coming of that other form of horsepower, motorised transport, that meant the passing of an era although horses worked alongside the new lorries for two years before they were finally phased out. By the time that the Great War was over, the value of motor lorries and trucks had come to be appreciated. Many companies took advantage of war surplus vehicles and invested in this new form of transport. Wars are horrid, but they often provide spin offs that see technological development that they helped to accelerate. It is a case of needs must. So it was with the internal combustion engine. Huge strides were made in those war years so that equipment and troops could be moved more quickly. When peacetime came, business was quick to build on those lessons. Those that failed to see where the future lay went to the wall. The family was farsighted enough to recognised the way forward.

another branch of the family. Willis Askey had worked in timber felling and some of the early business the company carried out involved the movement of large amounts of wood to the sawmills. Everyone mucked in together. Grandparents toiled alongside youngsters in a real family manner. Gradually, the business developed into general haulage work and it was a local company, Wraggs and Marshalls, that provided much of the early trade. Equipment that was transported included long ceramic pipes and equipment for the Sheffield steel smelting industries. The yard at Loxley was a hive of activity as the family strove hard to keep pace with the amount of work coming their way. Naturally, although very reliable, the horses could only work slowly. There

Askey Transport continued to grow, even during the depression days of the late 1920s and early 1930s. During the second world war the business was ready to move on. Glass Tilt House had served its purpose.

***Above and top:*** *Some of the company's wagons decked out for early Whitsun celebrations.*

With the second half of the 20th century beckoning, it was time to move on to bigger things. By now, Harold Askey (Charlotte and Willis' son), together with his wife Phillis (the local policeman's daughter) had taken the family reins and the company's name had changed once more to H Askey. In April 1942, he oversaw the relocation to Confluence House, Malin Bridge. This was the site of a garage and filling station that had once been an old coaching station house. From this new base, Harold was able to expand the company's interests and activities even further. The company took over the business of the filling station, but with pressure given by the government on fuel at the time, this proved to be only ever a sideline. The company also began another venture into vehicle repairs which continued throughout the next move to Middlewood Road. Diversify or die became the slogan of the 1950s. As Britain got back on its feet after the war, Harold Askey made sure that the business was at the cutting edge. The variety of people he contracted for included carrying for local firms, as before, but it now included local authority work. Askey

**Above:** *Charlotte and Willis Askey.* **Right:** *Harold Askey with a company vehicle being used as a breakdown truck.* **Below:** *The company's first truck at Wraggs, who supplied the company with a lot of its early trade. The company has recently been closed.*

snowploughs kept the roads clear for road users during bitter Yorkshire winters. It amused him that his ploughs were also making way for Askey Transport lorries to carry on their trade. He was being paid for something from which his business would also benefit. The irony was not lost on him. It was an example of a canny business brain and made good sense. Local steel works were kept supplied, the mines got their pit props and Askey Transport continued to prosper.

Harold moved into the private hire and taxi business during this period. Wedding cars, parties and outings were catered for. Alongside this enterprise, he added a vehicle service and repair business to complement the transport services his company supplied. Over the years, transport of one form or another has been the bedrock of the family's success. However, it has always been careful enough to recognise the changing needs of its customers as well as the differences and developments in the local industrial and business community. Askey Transport has always been more than capable of adapting.

In addition to being able to change gradually with the times, the Askey family has acted swiftly and decisively when it has been needed. In 1958, just as the country had turned the corner from the lean postwar years and was prospering under the Macmillan 'never had it so good' government, the Askeys were given a jolt. The Malin Bridge lease, that had 10 years to run, was dramatically brought to Harold Askey's attention. Out of the blue, he was given an ultimatum. Buy up the lease or leave the premises within the week. The Askeys, although shocked by the sudden news, acted promptly. Refusing to bow to pressure, before the seven days were out the family had packed up home and business lock, stock and two smoking barrels. Assisting Harold at that time was his future son-in-law Ray Green. A new home was found in Ferriby Road and new business premises were found at Middlewood Road and the move was completed in 1959. All the business and family possessions were loaded onto a convoy of Askey lorries and the transition made swiftly and smoothly to the new base of operations. Middlewood Road was the site of Arundel Motors. Harold bought the company out and, once more, petrol and motor maintenance lived hand in hand with haulage and transport. Today it is a limited company, reflecting its rise in success.

Middlewood Road, although at the time a necessary move, was restricted and the firm found that despite its desire to expand, it couldn't. Another move took place in June 1988 to the firm's larger current premises at Livesey Street, which took it back to the banks of the Loxley river. Since that time the company has seen further expansion and success. Harold's three children have all played a key part in this success. Jean entered the business in the early 1960s working part time, finally focusing her full time attention on it in 1969. Steve came along next, and although there was a small gap when he left the company to

become a coach driver, he has been back with the family firm for over twenty years. Alan came into the company to take charge in 1972 following his father's death. Alan had been an apprentice with Leyland Albion, but had kept abreast of the family business by occasionally filling in when his father was on holiday. It has been Alan and Jean who have remained at the helm for around 30 years. They have helped continue the family traditions of good business sense and practicality.

Today, the company has given up its car repair business and with the premises at Livesey Street offering more space, the firm now runs a warehousing facility, storing anything from business directories to machinery. Also the firm has been able to diversify into artics as well as the original rigids. This was made possible by the space afforded at Livesey Street. There is now another generation working for the company, with Jean's son, Garry, and Alan's son, Robert, showing a keen interest in the fortunes of the company that was started almost a century before their birth.

*Top: Arundel Garage at Middlewood Street, purchased in 1959. **Above Right:** St George and the Dragon on the side of one of the company's current lorrys. **Right:** A line-up of some of Askey's fleet of vehicles. Most of the fleet are rigids.*

# Going to the Dogs!

How many readers of this book have visited the Sheffield Sports Stadium? There can be very few long-time residents of the city who have not, at one time or another, been along to the Owlerton stadium.

There can be few experiences which stick in one's mind more than the thrill of attending one's first speedway race: the noise of the crowd, the tannoy system, and the tension. But above all is the memory of the roar of the engines from the four motor cycles as their riders compete for position as they hurtle round the narrow track amid the all pervading smell of 'dope', the high octane fuel used in the machines. And how many of us can forget standing too close to the barrier in our foolish youth and receiving a faceful of cinders as the riders skidded round the corners of the track only feet from our eyes?

The magnificent sporting venue that stands at Owlerton today is a long way from the simple dreams of the small band of Sheffield speedway enthusiasts whose members clubbed together in 1929 to promote the then new spectacle of speedway riding, the exciting American sport which had recently arrived in Yorkshire via Australia. The intrepid band of motorcyclists chose for their race track the water meadow amongst the Alder trees ('Owler' in the Anglo-Saxon) at the confluence of the Rivers Don and Loxley to the north side of the city. Unbeknown to the speedway pioneers however they were following in the tracks of a variety of sportsmen and promoters who had already used the village green for many purposes down the decades.

Most famous perhaps of all the world's showmen, Colonel William F 'Buffalo Bill' Cody, brought his renowned Wild West Show and Congress of Rough Riders to Owlerton in 1891. It took three railway trains to transport the 600 Indians, cowboys, Cossacks and Arabs and their 500 horses. The renowned Annie Oakley was the sharp shooting star of the show and gave her legendary performance demonstrating her unique brand of marksmanship (or perhaps in these politically correct times that should be markswomanship?) and in the process acquiring a fame of such proportion that many of today's youngsters if asked would doubt her existence as a real rather than fictional personality.

**Above:** *A poster advertising the annual sports event at Owlerton in 1899.*
**Below:** *Greyhounds being exercised in 1932.*

"News of the World" National Inter-Track Greyhound Racing Finals at Clapton. 22nd November. 1951. (Clapton v. Owlerton, Sheffield. Won by Owlerton)

Wyoming. Sadly on their visit to Owlerton two of Buffalo Bill's Red Indians ended up with an unscheduled journey to the Happy Hunting Grounds: they may have survived an encounter with General Custer but Sheffield proved their nemesis and they are buried in the cemetery opposite the stadium - illness rather than bullets from Colonel Cody's silver-plated six-guns was however the cause of their demise.

For years afterwards the 'Green' was known as Buffalo Bill's Field and annual athletic meetings were organised there carrying substantial cash prizes in the years before the stadium was built. Speedway alone however was unable to support the high running costs of the stadium and greyhound racing was introduced in 1932, and since then has never ceased to provide excitement and spectacle regularly three times a week.

In addition to the excitement generated by Miss Oakley and a host of other performers the Deadwood Stage provided a wild Western all action finale, being chased around the green by a large band of wildly whooping genuine Red Indians before the stage coach and its passengers were finally rescued by the US cavalry led by the man on the white horse, Buffalo Bill himself. Cody having seen off the Indian hordes rode his horse atop an artificial mountain, hat in hand, to take the crowd's cheers and applause whilst his magnificent mount, rearing on its hind legs, pawed the air.

Hard though it is to believe, only fifteen years earlier some of those same Indians whom William Cody had driven off in his stage-managed war had participated in Custer's Last Stand, immortalised on film on so many occasions, when General George Armstrong Custer had led the US 6th cavalry to annihilation by the Sioux Indian nation in the grassy hills above the Little Big Horn River in

***Top:*** *A floodlit stadium in 1932.*
***Above left:*** *Intertrack greyhound racing final between Clapton and Owlerton in November 1951, won for Owlerton by Mad Astley.*
***Right:*** *A cartoon of a Speedway meeting in 1930.*

As a multi-purpose venue the stadium can be turned around to accommodate most sports: roller skating was a regular fixture in the 1930s and similarly pony racing gave paying customers the thrills and spills more usually associated, though on larger scale, with Doncaster, Pontefract and York.

One great opportunity associated with the stadium that died with the outbreak of the second world war was baseball. The Sheffield Dons baseball team captained by their Canadian pitcher Len Randle topped their league. Baseball is still played today in Hull and south Wales; perhaps a rebirth in Sheffield is overdue to get today's youngsters out from in front of the telly and into the fresh air. Who knows what might have happened had baseball continued to be played in Sheffield? Perhaps we would have no need of football, rugby and cricket to inspire local sports lovers and instead we would be glued to our televisions and papers desperate to discover how the Dons were faring against teams from New York, Chicago and Los Angeles; does anyone out there fancy backing a Sheffield team for the baseball World Series next year?

Perhaps more people have passed through the gates of the Sheffield Sports Stadium to watch the greyhound racing than for any other purpose. Greyhound racing had begun seven years before the start of the second world war and immediately attracted large attendances to watch what was often thought of as the 'poor mans horse racing'. Racing with dogs rather than horses may have been less expensive than a day out at Ascot but it was always just as much fun for the people of Sheffield - and a jolly sight easier to get to. Even though dog racing

began in the depression years of the 1930s there was still enough interest and money about to ensure that the sport was well supported and income to keep the stadium in business was maintained.

Many people have a flutter on the horses but have never seen a live horse race; the same is far less true of dog racing. A night at the dogs was always an event, and betting, whether for small or large amounts, an essential part of the immense pleasure which its supporters gave to the races. No-one who has ever placed a bet at the dog track will ever forget their disappointment at losing their stake the first time they paced a bet - or, if they were lucky,

***Top:*** *An England v Sweden international heat in June 1973 which was won by Ray Wilson.*
***Above:*** *Three of the greatest litter - Tric Trac, Spectre and Forward King in 1967.*

siblings Forward King and Forward Flash who also took all before them. Some things happen only once in a lifetime; it is doubtful that a single litter will produce so many champion dogs again in the lifetime of those who saw those dogs run.

In recent years Owlerton has taken the National Intertrack Competition twice and looks forward to the future with confidence. Visitors attending the stadium who have been there before will however always be reminded of happy years gone by, of famous wins, losses and crashes at the Speedway; of fabulous greyhounds which lost them money or, in winning, gave us stories with which to regale our grandchildren. And although none now living may now recall seeing Buffalo Bill and Annie Oakley at Owlerton perhaps visitors may sometimes spare a thought in their direction too.

the intense joy of winning, even if they had placed no more than a tanner on the dog of their choice.

There are few grander sights than seeing a greyhound, a supreme athlete, racing around a track in competition with other dogs in similar condition. The Sheffield Stadium seems to have always provided just a little more excitement than other venues as the greyhounds raced around its big sweeping bends. Its atmosphere is unique.

Naturally over the years many greyhounds became famous and their proud owners would treat their dogs like royalty, feeding them on nothing but the best - no living off leftovers and scraps like lesser mutts. Famous dogs came and went throughout the decades then along came 1967 and four extraordinary greyhounds from the same litter, no doubt the finest litter ever born and which went on to sweep the board - Sheffield Greyhound fans of the period will never forget Tric Trac who won the Derby - Spectre II who won the St Leger and their

***Top (both pictures):*** *Willie Harrison, Rotherham's world champion Stockcar driver.*
***Above left:*** *A promotional shot for Owlerton stadium taken in 1969, full of familiar faces!*
***Below:*** *The Master and Mistress Cutler, Mr and Mrs Paul J Tear admire the Red Mills Supertrack trophy won in 1997 and 98.*

# *Putting a shine on Sheffield*

Sheffield may have created a name for itself through its steel production and its silver plate; but silver is not the only metal which can be used to coat other metals. Chromium, cadmium, copper, nickel, tin and zinc can all be applied to other materials using similar electroplating processes. Initially in demand for purely decorative purposes electroplating and its associated skills are now in demand for a whole range of industrial applications: one Sheffield firm which has an admirable and long-standing reputation in the field is Stainless Plating Ltd.

Stainless Plating was incorporated as a limited company on 3rd September 1926 as a business specialising in decorative chrome electroplating and industrial hard chrome plating.

At its inception the firm traded from the Chrome Plate Works, Brown Street, Sheffield, near to the city centre and quickly became one of the major electroplating companies in Yorkshire.

**Right:** *Harry Bottom, left of lamp post, outside the Sheffield Furnishing Company on London Road.*
**Below:** *Polishing car radiators as well as hospital cupboard frames.*

The main processes carried out were Nickel and Chromium plating although at one stage the firm's Hard Chromium plating facilities processed the largest items ever plated in Europe: a series of steel rollers fourteen feet long and weighing two and a half tons each.

Always involved in quality electroplating the firm's earliest 'approval' was awarded by the Good Housekeeping Institute in 1928 for its chromium plated steel products.

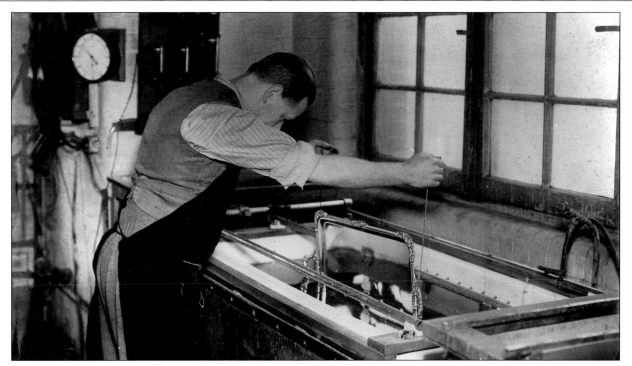

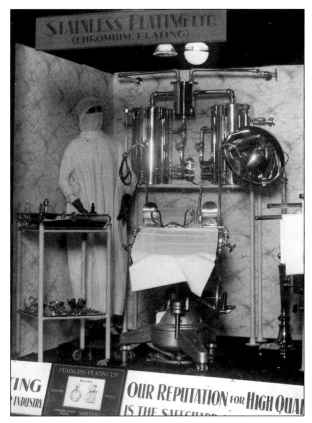

In June 1954 the company was purchased by the late Harry Bottom. Harry Bottom had actually retired in 1937, at the age of 49, having sold his very successful business, the Sheffield Furnishing Company in London Road, to John Blundell Ltd a company based in London. On the outbreak of war Harry Bottom came out of retirement and returned to Sheffield from the south of England, initially buying Roper and Wreakes Ltd an engineering company and clutch manufacturer. He went onto acquire several other businesses.

In November 1956 Harry Bottom bought the electro-plating business of Sheffield's William Bowker and Sons Ltd whose main activity was silver plating. During the war that firm too had diversified into similar processes to those carried out by Stainless Plating Ltd and it also held similar approvals. It was however a much older established company having been founded in 1889. William Bowker & Sons had initially occupied premises in Orchard Lane, Sheffield and had been based there for fourteen years before moving to Carver Street where it remained until 1958. When it was purchased by Harry Bottom all Bowker's facilities were transferred to Stainless Plating's Brown Street works with the exception of silver plating which, because of the lack of space, was moved to premises at 54a Staveley Road, Sheffield and continued to trade from there as William Bowker & Sons Ltd plating traditional Sheffield holloware and cutlery.

Rather than operating from two premises however it was later decided to enlarge the factory space at Staveley Road, where the existing premises had actually been built in 1882. Stainless Plating and its facilities were moved there.

During the second world war much of the business' facilities were turned over to other forms of processing required for the war effort particularly Parkerising, cadmium plating, tin plating and silver plating. As far back as 1937 the company had been approved by the Air Ministry (later to become the Ministry of Aviation) and subsequently gained approval by the Ministry of Supply and Defence's Quality Assurance Board. On the civilian side approval was also gained from the Air Registration Board (later to become the Civil Aviation Authority).

*Left: An early Stainless Plating Ltd stand at the Sheffield Industries Exhibition. Top: Rhodium Plating.*

The move was made in 1966. Both companies now traded under the sole name of Stainless Plating Ltd.

By the early 1990s the company was coming under increasing pressure from new environmental legislation which it was finding difficult to comply with. Coupled with that problem the company had also outgrown its premises and plans were made to move to a completely new site.

The latest change of location was completed in November 1996 when the company moved into its present purpose built premises at 24 Don Road, Sheffield on the Newhall Riverside Estate of the Lower Don Valley. Ninety-five per cent of the processing facilities was of new manufacture and every conceivable

**Right:** *Polishing a chromium plated steel roller weighing 3 tons.*
**Top:** *A group of polishers after a days work.*

environmentally friendly option was included. The company currently has a workforce of twenty-five employees.

Today the company is a subsidiary of Harry Bottom (Holdings) Ltd which is in turn owned by the Harry Bottom Charitable Trust. The trust was set up by Harry Bottom as a self perpetuating trust, the income generated being used for the benefit of medical, religious and general charitable causes.

During the years since the company was acquired by Harry Bottom it has been almost continuously changing to meet the requirements of its customers. As new technology and materials have evolved the call for certain finishes has diminished. In those cases the processing capacity has been rationalised or dispensed with entirely to make room for newer process requirements to meet the demand for new finishes.

Besides producing a passive surface on the components it also produces a surface free of both contamination and imbedded particles of foreign materials.

With the advent of BS 5750 (subsequently BS EN ISO 9002) many commercial customers now require work processed to agreed standards through the use of process specifications. This generally causes no problems as the company's extensive library contains over 1500 different specifications.

One thing that has changed is that the company no longer silver plates for the traditional local trades. i.e. cutlery and holloware. The silver plating facility now caters for the plating of high precision engineering components which require a pure form of plating solutions with no brighteners or additives and includes work for the nuclear industry.

Providing a service to the aerospace industry has always remained of paramount importance to the company and approvals have been obtained from firms such as Rolls Royce, British Aerospace, Lucas Aerospace, Normalair-Garrett, Raytheon Corporate Jets, Dowty Defence & Air Systems and Short Brothers to name but a few. To cater for those clients' exacting requirements improved testing facilities have been installed. Various forms of equipment for the testing of deposit thickness are now used - both destructive and non-destructive. Accelerated corrosion test equipment has also been added to the firm's facilities including salt spray and humidity cabinets.

Two of the latest pieces of equipment acquired are an X-ray fluorescence spectrometer used to non-destructively determine multi-layer coating thickness and analyse metals and solutions as well as an instrument using polarography and voltammetry which can detect substances in solutions at concentrations lower than one part per billion. This latter piece of equipment is used to ensure that the company complies with trade effluent discharge limits set as low as fifty parts per billion.

Concurrent with re-equipping, the development of the general commercial side of the business has continued. Blasting of components, either as a pre-treatment or a post treatment, can now be carried out in any of four wet or dry blasting facilities. Methods of masking components are continually improving as is the handling of components during processing by the acquisition of better jigs.

With the increased use of corrosion resistant steels, modern plant, complete with air extraction, has been installed over the past few years to enable the company to offer stainless steel passivation facilities.

With the move to new premises improvements have also been made in the efficient use of resources with heated tanks thermostatically controlled and suitably insulated to take advantage of economy fuel rates. In addition, operating practices have been changed where lower temperatures or lower concentrations of solutions have been found beneficial. Improved rinsing and handling of work has also led to improved efficiency both by reducing effluent treatment costs and by the extended use of reclaimed materials

The company has also made every effort to ensure that it offers a safe working environment to its employees and has complied with all the changes required by Health & Safety legislation. So safety conscious has the company been that when the 'COSHH' regulations were introduced virtually no operational change was required when the assessment was carried out. All employees are provided with regular examinations by a doctor specialising in Occupational Health to ensure that the environment in which they work imposes no risks their health.

For three quarters of a century Stainless Plating Ltd has met the demands of its clients by continuously moving forward to embrace the latest in modern technology. Much has changed since 1926 but one thing remains the same: a commitment to the highest standards of craftsmanship in a highly specialist field.

**Top left:** *Hi-tech plating facilities on Don Road.*
**Below:** *The current premises.*

# *Packing for posterity*

Used as we now are to seeing goods packaged in cardboard boxes and nestling securely in plastic and polystyrene it takes some effort to recall that not so long ago loose dry goods, as well as liquids of all kinds, were normally transported from place to place in barrels. One company which not only knows about today's state of the art packaging methods but also about the history of packing is the renowned Sheffield packaging firm of W K West Limited, based at its fully-equipped premises in Cornish Street.

The West packaging business can be traced back as far as 1816, the year following the Duke of Wellington's glorious victory over Napoleon Bonapart at the Battle of Waterloo, and to the small cooperage firm of T & W Raine which was founded in that year.

The real story however begins in 1884 when William Kershaw West acquired the Raine dry coopering business. At that time barrels made by dry coopers were in particular demand for transporting the many types of files and hand tools produced in Sheffield for export. Mechanical handling being unknown in many foreign ports meant that barrels, which could be easily rolled, were understandably popular with many overseas buyers.

William West was the son of a master brass-founder and William had followed that trade himself until he decided to set up his own business at the age of twenty-five.

Doing well for himself in his new business venture William West moved to the firm's present site in Cornish Street in about 1889 - an early outward symbol of success was having a telephone installed, with the number Sheffield 721. In the final decade of the 19th century the business was advertising itself as W K West, Cooper and Packing Case Manufacturer. The firm offered to supply clients with all kinds of wood and metal cases and boxes in addition to a wide range of barrels ranging from those of under a dozen gallons capacity to huge casks capable of holding over two hundred gallons.

The firm's founder was joined around 1910 by his son William Morgan prior to him being called up for service during the first world war and a second son, Kenneth William West, joined the firm in 1925. The business continued to grow and became a limited company in 1920; at around the same time an additional area was added to the premises to cope with the growing demand.

The business continued to grow through the most difficult times: shortages of materials and staff during two world wars caused enormous problems for the firm whilst the interwar slump of the 1930s saw the demand for packing products go into a serious decline. In the 1920s the Wests had even diversified and bought an asphalters. Despite those inevitable fluctuations in trade however the firm continued to expand and by the 1940s was employing around thirty employees. Also, in 1940, the company had to come to terms with the death of it's founder WK West. A third generation of the family, James Gordon West, William M West's son, joined the firm in 1947.

Lessons learned in improved material handling during the war were now being absorbed by shipping companies with the result that lighter forms of packaging were called for.

**Top left:** *William Kershaw West, founder of the company.* **Above:** *A packing case and barrel price list from 1892.*

---

TELEPHONE No 721.

## W. K. WEST,

### Cooper and Packing Case Maker,

MANUFACTURER OF ALL KINDS OF

WOOD, TIN AND ZINC CASES, SAW BOARDS, BOXES, &c., &c.

### CASK LIST.—1892.

| GALLONS | PRICE £ s. d. | GALLONS | PRICE £ s. d. | GALLONS | PRICE £ s. d. |
|---|---|---|---|---|---|
| **4 Hoops.** | | **6 Hoops** | | 123 to 127 | 1 2 0 |
| 13 & under 14, 15, | 0 5 6 | 43 to 47 | 0 13 6 | 128 to 132 | 1 2 6 |
| 16, 17, | 0 6 6 | 48 to 52 | 0 14 0 | 133 to 137 | 1 3 0 |
| 18, 19, 20, | 0 7 0 | 53 to 57 | 0 14 6 | 138 to 142 | 1 3 6 |
| 21, 22, 23, | 0 8 0 | 58 to 62 | 0 15 0 | 143 to 147 | 1 4 0 |
| 24, 25, 26, | 0 8 6 | 63 to 67 | 0 15 6 | 148 to 152 | 1 4 6 |
| 27, 28, 29, | 0 9 0 | 68 to 72 | 0 16 0 | 153 to 157 | 1 5 0 |
| 30, 31, 32, | 0 9 6 | 73 to 77 | 0 16 6 | 158 to 162 | 1 5 6 |
| 33 34 35. | 0 10 0 | 78 to 82 | 0 17 0 | 163 to 167 | 1 6 0 |
| 36, 37, 38, | 0 10 6 | 83 to 87 | 0 17 6 | 168 to 172 | 1 6 6 |
| 39, 40, | 0 11 0 | 88 to 92 | 0 18 0 | 173 to 177 | 1 7 0 |
| **6 Hoops.** | | 93 to 97 | 0 18 6 | 178 to 182 | 1 7 6 |
| | | 98 to 102 | 0 19 0 | 183 to 187 | 1 8 0 |
| 30, 31, 32, | 0 11 0 | 103 to 107 | 1 0 0 | 188 to 192 | 1 8 6 |
| 33, 34, | 0 11 6 | 108 to 112 | 1 0 6 | 193 to 197 | 1 9 0 |
| 35, 36, 37, | 0 12 6 | 113 to 117 | 1 1 0 | 198 to 202 | 1 9 6 |
| 33 to 42 | 0 13 0 | 118 to 122 | 1 1 6 | | |

| FILE CASKS. | £ s. d. | NETT PRICE OF CASK LININGS. | |
|---|---|---|---|
| 7 Cwt. 6 Hoops and Bars | 0 9 6 | | |
| 8 " | 0 10 6 | TIN | per foot. |
| 9 " | 0 11 0 | | |
| 10 " | 0 11 6 | ZINC | per foot. |
| 11 " | 0 12 0 | | |
| 12 " | 0 12 6 | | |

All kinds of Casks and Cases made to order.

### CORNISH STREET, SHEFFIELD.

It became apparent that whilst solid wood packing cases would still be required a new market was opening up for lighter packing. As a consequence West's decided to extend the range of packaging materials offered and the 'Westply' metal edged plywood case was introduced. Consisting of plywood panels linked by metal edging attached by rivets this method of construction provided an immensely strong but light method of packing goods.

Throughout the 1950s West's was kept busy making packing cases suited to the needs of all Sheffield trades - steel, small tools, saws - including circular saws, machinery and heavy engineering products; by the mid 1960s the heavy side of the business was increasing even more rapidly than the lighter side. Remarkably one of the special features of the business at this time however was that practically everything in the way of cases and crates had to be made within twenty-four hours, and often much less, and that the cases were all made to special order, frequently as single items.

By 1964 one entire department was being devoted exclusively to the production of Westply metal edged plywood cases. A sawing machine had been installed in which plywood panels could be gripped automatically in a pneumatic cramping device and then cut by a circular saw which rose from below. In that same department were machines that rapidly riveted the plywood box bottoms and sides to their metal edging. The noise of machinery must have seemed deafening in comparison to the pre-electric days when hand tools had been the order of the day: the older members of the workforce must have been astonished at the changes which had been wrought in just a few decades.

Other plant in the workshops included a range of more conventional sawing-machines incorporating circular-saws and bandsaws, 'thicknessers', boxboard printing machines, grooving and tonguing machines, multiple nailing machines and equipment for shearing and forming tinplate for the lining of waterproof cases and for soldering the formed linings.

*Top:* West's workers standing beside a wooden crate in 1953. **Above left:** *William Morgan West.* **Above right:** *Kenneth William West.* **Above centre:** *James Gordon West.*

By the mid 1960s the two West brothers and WM West's son James Gordon were the firm's three directors. In 1965 the company was appointed fabricators under licence for the American-developed packaging material Tri-Wall Pak. The material was a weight-saving triple-wall corrugated paper board which could replace timber in many packaging applications. James West soon demonstrated his confidence in the new material, investing £6,000 in special machinery to turn Tri Wall Pak into containers.

James West had good reason to have confidence in the new corrugated board: its strength was spectacularly demonstrated at Niagara Falls in 1976 by the material's manufacturers Tri-Wall Containers Ltd. To prove how strong its material was the company launched five containers made from the special material over the Niagara falls.

England's Captain Webb, the first man to swim the English Channel, had famously drowned trying to swim the rapids below the falls; others had died going over Niagara in barrels; but the water's terrible reputation did not deter the Tri-Wall Pak company.

Each package contained a cargo of delicate Royal

*Right: West's provided the packing case to transport what was the largest mirror in the UK, to an equestrian centre. **Top left:** An advertisement for Westply plywood cases.*

Brierley crystal glass surrounded by dry rock salt. Two of the containers simply disappeared in the boiling torrent but in the three which were retrieved the glass was unbroken and not a single grain of salt was dampened. Tri-wall Containers Ltd and W K West Ltd lost no time in pointing out that this extraordinary publicity stunt provided even further assurance for customers who left their containers exposed to all weathers, or exported them as deck cargo through the worst storm conditions.

Following the deaths of the founder's two sons in the early 1970s the firm diversified with distributorships in self-adhesive tape, cushioning material and plastic strapping systems.

Major expansion took place from about 1980 when property became available around the site. In September 1980 the firm announced completion of

an extensive new warehouse which enabled it to offer a wider range of heavy duty corrugated cases for immediate delivery. The new warehouse adjoining the existing plant was used to hold both Tri-wall Pak and Doublewall corrugated cases and sheet stocks for the manufacture of stock size containers.

In 1995 the firm acquired the Midland Box Company Ltd at Kirkby in Ashfield providing the ability to supply lighter grade cardboard - and simultaneously beginning the WK West group of companies. Today up to date automated machinery and power tools have greatly improved working methods and conditions in the factory. The firm also has a range of modern company vehicles and delivers goods using its own liveried transport - the

*Top: A large crate, manufactured by WK West, loaded onto a local delivery firm's truck.*
*Above: One of WK West's current fleet of vehicles.*
*Right: A busy hi-tech sales office.*

white lorries with their bright orange West logo are frequently seen making deliveries around Sheffield and further afield throughout Yorkshire, Derbyshire, Lincolnshire and the North Midlands.

Currently the firm's fifty or so employees are divided amongst two sites and three separate trading divisions: West Packaging is concerned with corrugated cases, cushioning material, strapping systems, wooden products and general packaging materials, West Tapes retails and distributes specialist technical tapes whilst most recently the company has launched an Internet on-line trading division - Express Packaging.

James West retired from his role as managing director in 1996 but remains as company chairman. In more than a century of involvement with the packaging industry the West family can look back with astonishment and pride that the small cooperage and packing firm bought by William Kershaw West in 1884 is going strong and able to look forward to the future with confidence.

# *Read all about it...*

**W**e take it for granted that our daily newspapers will be delivered to our local newsagents and from there to our letter boxes without a hitch. We are unlikely to spare much thought to the complex distribution network which it is necessary to maintain in order to perform this daily miracle. One of the most important parts of that difficult process is performed by Sheffield's H Turner & Son Ltd.

The Turner story began in early 1891 when Harry Turner, a one-time left luggage porter who had later served an informal apprenticeship with two Sheffield newsagents, set up in business for himself in Sheffield's Bank Street.

Harry Turner occupied numbers 13 and 15 Bank Street and advertised his services as a printer, publisher and bookbinder - and only secondarily as a newsagent and stationer. The business was soon a success: by 1898 Harry had a second shop in South Street, Sheffield Moor and soon another in Cumberland Street before selling them to buy city centre premises in the High Street, premises which were in turn sold on in the 1920s.

From those small beginnings grew the firm of H Turner & Son Ltd one of England's foremost wholesale and retail newsagents and one which would eventually employ over a thousand people in a network which until recent times included more than a hundred newsagents shops.

The firm's story spans five generations of the same family. Harry Turner, the firm's founder, built a profitable though small scale business which was making a very healthy £1,000 profit in 1920.

**Above left:** *An early advertisement.*
**Above right:** *Harry Turner.*
**Below:** *Turner's shop in 1911.*

Harry's son, Archie, did little to change the business merely keeping things as they were at the time of his father's death in 1934 during which year the business actually recorded a loss of £51 despite an annual turnover in excess of £25,000.

It was Gordon Harry Bryars Turner, the founder's grandson, who, full of ambition, saw the potential for expansion and began the dramatic growth of the business into both new shops and wholesale activities.

At the beginning of the 1930s the young Gordon Turner had been sent to Abel Heyward & Son Ltd in Manchester as an apprentice. Abel Heyward had been in existence for over a century and had grown in that period into a famous name in news agency and stationery. In 1934, shortly before his grandfathers death, brimming with ideas and enthusiasm, Gordon returned to Sheffield to join the family firm.

Inheriting a large proportion of his grandfather's shares in the firm, it fell to Gordon to make Turners into the large and nationally established business which it is today. In 1937 the Bank Street premises were completely refurbished and the adjoining number

17 was acquired for expansion. Only those who knew the previous premises could have had an idea of the transformation which took place. Instead of just two small windows to the shop there were now three spacious well stocked windows in Bank Street with a fourth in the fine entrance lobby. The growth in business however really started at the end of the second world war. One of Gordon's first enthusiasms was a move into greeting cards: the firm ended up becoming one of the largest wholesalers of greetings card in the country. Strangely, in view of the way the future turned out however Gordon always felt that wholesaling would not survive and so began expanding the retail business as early as 1940, leading eventually to the setting up of the chain of newsagents shops under the name of GT News.

Before that expansion however came the war. Gordon enlisted in the Royal Engineers - becoming a staff-sergeant. Gordon's military career was to be short-lived however being discharged on medical grounds in 1942 to face the twin problems of bomb damage to the

*Above: Archie Turner. **Top:** An early picture of the staff. **Right:** Turner's bombed Bank Street premises.*

Bank Street premises and a father who had lost all interest in the business following the tragically early death of his wife in 1940.

As a result of the German onslaught the warehouse and office at Bank Street had been gutted leaving only the stock room and the front shop standing - though with its windows not unsurprisingly shattered. Archie wrote to his son that he was considering asking W H Smith & Son to run the news business for the remainder of the war.

Less than six months after Gordon's return from the forces however things moved forward rapidly; he arranged to buy the Thompson news agency at 399 South Road Walkley. In the spring of 1945 Gordon bought a second shop, Foster's tobacconists and sweet shop at 59 Commercial Street at the entrance to the Rag Market which was to continue in business until the Rag Market itself closed in 1972.

The turnover of H Turner, separate from Gordon's other stores, continued to improve, business increasing

from an annual turnover of £37,000 in 1941 prior to Gordon's return to £95,000 by 1948.

The first signs of substantial post-war progress however was the move of the wholesale business to West Bar in 1947. Growth in business was so rapid that even those premises quickly became inadequate and by 1958 the adjoining Blue Boar pub was acquired. Soon however even that proved too small even though in 1957 the wholesale night news despatch operation was relocated to premises at Canal Wharf. The following year, 1959, a small piece of Sheffield's history ended when Turners ceased business from the original Bank Street premises when the area was vacated to make way for city centre redevelopment.

**Above:** *The warehouse in 1959.* **Top:** *The Castle Street shop in 1959.* **Left:** *Some of the company's early vehicles.*

Archie died 1962, a cautious, thoughtful man who appeared to have been astonished at the energy and enthusiasm, which in his view sometimes bordered on the reckless, that his son had brought to the family firm.

The Richmond Park Road building became the firm's headquarters in 1973 and placed the wholesale business under one roof. Moving to Richmond Park Road marked the start of another period of rapid growth and in the 1970s the firm acquired two of Barnsley's wholesale news agencies as well as launching into a major expansion of its retail shops with change, diversification and expansion evidenced by the establishment of GT Sports and the opening a first large store - the GT Leisuretime premises at Hillsborough.

In August 1948, even after Gordon Turner's early efforts at expansion, the firm however still employed only 23 staff, by 1952 that figure had grown to 52 and by the end of that decade 100. By the end of the 1960s it had topped 150. In the same period the number of newsagents being supplied by the firm had risen from 65 to over 150.

On Gordon's death in 1979 he left the firm well-equipped for further growth, handing on the family baton to Ashley Turner. Ashley had worked for WH Smith in Stoke on Trent from 1961 to 62 before returning to the family business in 1963 and worked in both the retail sector and the wholesale and news distribution before becoming a director in 1966. In 1989 Ashley relinquished his joint role as Chairman and chief executive and appointed Don Lyon as chief in his place. Don Lyon, Turners' current Chief Executive, had joined the firm in 1972 as retail controller.

By 1988 Turners were trading from a over a hundred news outlets and had a dozen GT Sports shops of which five were incorporated within GT news stores. In addition in the same year a group of nine shops were bought in the Coventry area.

By the early 1990s the company had grown to having over 1200 employees with growth aided by the acquisition of further newspaper distribution businesses in Guildford and Kings Cross, London. The chain was however eventually sold in 2000 to the Nottingham firm of A R Daunt & Co Ltd, wholesalers of tobacco and confectionery.

Ashley's son Ryck (the fifth generation of the family to be involved with the firm) served a three year apprenticeship with WH Smith and with a trade association before joining the company in 1995 as general manager of the news wholesaling business in Guildford. He was appointed a director of Turners News Ltd in 1996, joint managing director in 1998 and managing director in 1999 when he was also appointed to the main board of H Turner & Son Limited.

News distribution has moved to purpose designed and built premises on a 3.5 acre site at Europa Way. The 74,000 square feet premises represent an investment of £3 million and contains a computerised information system for the specialist distribution of papers and magazines. The business now concentrates solely on news and magazine wholesaling. Perhaps the next time we pick up our morning paper we will spare a thought for Henry Turner, a man whose efforts helped make that small daily miracle possible.

***Above left:*** *Ashley Turner.* **Below:** *The new Head Office and news distribution centre at Europa Drive.* **Bottom:** *West Bar premises.*

# A prescription for achievement

How many readers recall NHS prescription charges being introduced in 1952 - at a shilling (5p) per form? How much are they now? When the NHS had started in 1948 prescriptions had been free for everyone - and the government soon got an unpleasant shock when it discovered just how many prescriptions were being dispensed and at what cost to the exchequer. The cost of running the NHS was far greater than anyone had forecast and so prescription charges were one method of addressing the balance. Not everyone was happy, especially not Aneurin Bevan who had introduced the NHS, nor Yorkshireman and future Prime Minister Harold Wilson, both of whom resigned from the government in protest.

Of course not only patients and politicians were annoyed by the new charges, chemists who dispensed prescriptions and relied on them for their income were affected too as the number of forms presented fell in response to the charges being introduced. All in all the period was perhaps not an auspicious one in which to open a new pharmacy.

The Wicker is one of Sheffield's best known landmarks famous as the place 'weer t'watter runs oer t'weir'. The Wicker got its name from the basket weavers who once worked amongst the rushes on the banks of the Don. Today the most famous part of The Wicker is the building which houses Associated Chemists (Wicker) Ltd.

**Both pages:** *The shop and dispensary in the 1950s.*

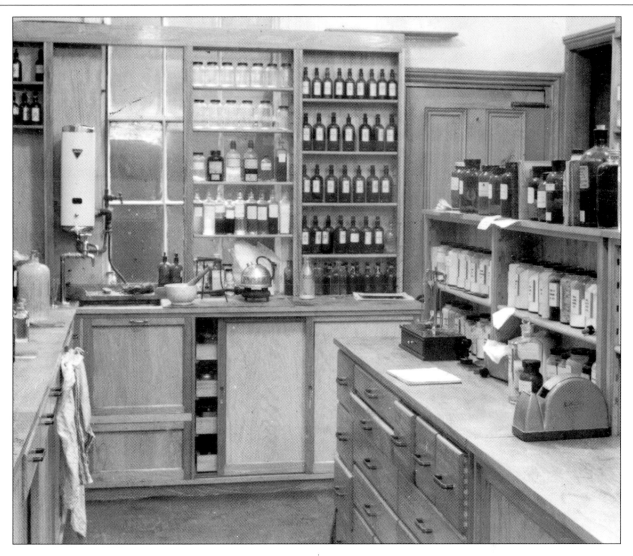

The company was formed on 25th June 1951 by 45 of the private chemists in the Sheffield area with the intention of jointly providing a late opening service in competition with Boots. This appears to have been the first consortium owned pharmacy in the country. The hours of opening were 9am to 10pm Monday to Saturday and 2pm to 8 pm on Sundays and Public Holidays. The company was the brainchild of Len Stocks who became its first Secretary alongside Chairman Cyril Hobson.

In 1977, looking back over the company's first 25 years, Len Stocks explained that 'the business was founded because local chemists felt frustrated when new NHS regulations required them to display the name of other competing pharmacies on their doors whenever they were shut and the competitor was open. Shareholders in the new pharmacy however were soon able to display in their windows a notice referring to the late opening service being given by 'our pharmacy' in the city centre in addition to their competitor.

The new company was formed with rules that only pharmacists and their immediate relatives could hold shares. The maximum shareholding was fixed at £500 and capital of £15,000 was soon raised from the 45 pharmacies joining in.

The holding of shares by each investor was limited to a maximum holding of 3.3 per cent of the share capital. Each shareholder would receive an annual dividend paid from expected profits.

By the time Len Stocks stepped down as secretary in 1972 he estimated that the shareholders had by then received dividends of more than four time their original investments.

Things did not go as smoothly as might be expected today however: building materials were in short supply and obtaining Ministry of Works licences for the building and shopfitting work was difficult. A permit for new floor boards was refused at first and an appeal was only successful after the certifying officer had been carefully steered over a particularly rotten section of floor.

The board of the new company had met for the first time on 19th July 1951 and the following month an advert had appeared in the Pharmaceutical Journal for a qualified pharmacist to act as managing director together with two qualified assistants.

Thomas Hall Turnbull of Galashiels was appointed superintendent pharmacist and managing director on a salary of £800 a year and the shop at 61 The Wicker

opened in February 1952 and has been open every day since then. Over the years the business has since expanded into numbers 63, 65, 69 and 71.

The initial concept was to employ three qualified staff but due to difficulty in recruiting pharmacists the pharmacy opened with the managing director working during the day whilst one of the seven directors would cover the evening and Sunday hours.

The novel development led to a number of similar but completely unconnected 'Associated Chemists' being set up in Birmingham, Stockport, Newcastle, Birkenhead and Wolverhampton. By the mid 1960s an editorial in the Pharmaceutical Journal was suggesting that this type of group practice could be the way for independent pharmacists to develop in city centres. Later a number of consortium pharmacies opened in or near health centres.

By 1973, 22 years after the company's foundation, annual turnover was £66,000 but the business made a small loss - further more the fixtures and fittings were becoming 'tired' and needed replacing. A complete refit was undertaken to provide what was then a quite futuristic pharmacy - turnover had increased significantly to £240,000 by 1979 when 63 ad 65 Wicker were purchased. 70 per cent of turnover however was from NHS dispensing. That proportion had increased gradually over the previous decade effecting all independent pharmacies - in some cases rising from around 50 per cent of income to over 80 per cent. Although the company still saw its role as primarily providing a professional dispensing service the fact that almost

all its eggs were in one basket - the government's - was a little worrying. Subsequent developments showed that such concern was all too real and diversification became the order of the day. Having been so heavily dependant upon NHS dispensing the business expanded into wheelchairs and rehabilitation equipment eventually becoming Handicapped Living Centre, later renamed "HLC - Sheffield Mobility Shop" which by 1985 was to occupy 69-71 of the Wicker and in 1987 number 67 too.

In 1980 a car park for 14 cars at the junction of Andrew Street and the Wicker was acquired and in 1983 a further car park at the rear of 61 Wicker for six cars; meanwhile maximum benefit was gained from the upper floors by letting one out as a dental surgery and another as a four bedroomed flat.

***Above:*** *Wilberforce Hotel and the pharmacy in the 1960s.* ***Top:*** *Cyril Hobson, the first Chairman in 1951.*

with local health service providers developing a number of new initiatives such as the supply of patient information leaflets with prescribed medicines, an award winning method of dispensing medication for patients who have difficulty in managing their tablets called Medicine-on-Time, a "touch screen" information system for customers to access and an Internet website (www.wicker.co.uk). Close links with drug treatment clinics have allowed an improved system of monitored supply to be introduced and the company has been instrumental in developing a network of pharmacists undertaking research into community pharmacy practice. HLC - Sheffield Mobility Shop has built on its' earlier successes so that it is now recognised as one of the most comprehensively equipped showrooms for specialist equipment in the country with a home demonstration and installation service that covers most of the north of England. In addition H+H System continues to supply both hospital and community pharmacies throughout the country with specialised fittings for the storage of pharmaceuticals.

During the late 1980s opportunities were sought to expand the business further: another Handicapped Living Centre was opened in Hull in 1988 whilst another pharmacy was opened in Grenoside in 1989. Another pharmacy offering late night services was opened in Hull in 1990 and one in Sheffield's Prince of Wales Road was bought in 1992. The Grenoside and Prince of Wales Road pharmacies were however soon sold again.

From 1988 the firm also marketed the Austrian 'H+H System' of dividers for drawers, shelves and fridges.

By 1993 the group turnover was a hefty £2.5 million but a policy decision was made to return to 'grass roots' and the outlets in Hull were sold. By the end of 1993 the company was once again trading exclusively from the Wicker site. In the pharmacy modifications were made to create a counselling area and a separate room for Care Home Dispensing whilst provision was made for Healthcall Ltd, the Doctors' Deputising Service, to use part of the premises as an emergency surgery for a trial period.

Associated Chemists continued to be at the forefront of pharmacy developments with the three divisions, all based on the Wicker, trading successfully throughout the nineties. Ownership of the Company itself remained in the hands of 34 pharmacist shareholders. The pharmacy continued to forge close links

As the company's fiftieth birthday approaches, one wonders whether the original shareholders, when launching the country's first "consortium pharmacy", envisaged that, by the turn of the century, it would have dispensed over 4 million NHS prescriptions and would be employing over 50 staff.

Surprisingly ever increasing prescription charges have failed to curb demand: from a national figure of 100 million prescriptions a year in the early days of the NHS the number now exceeds 540 million each year a goodly proportion dispensed in Sheffield - one can only wonder how high the figure would have become if prescription changes had never been introduced.

**Above left:** *The pharmacy today.*
**Below:** *Wicker, home of Associated Chemists.*

# X-ray vision

In December 1994 the Sheffield firm of T W Sampson & Co Electrical Engineers and Contractors moved to new premises at Frecheville House in Birley Moor Road. Had the long-established business stayed put for just another nine months the company could have celebrated sixty years of occupation of its Electron Works in Pitt Street.

It was early in September 1935 that T W Sampson took the ground floor of the premises in Pitt Street naming it the Electron Works. The premises had been used previously as a garage but from the gullies in the floor it had certainly been stables before that. The upper floor was at that time used as a Gospel Hall. The firm's first task was to build an office, store and a workshop area.

T W Sampson was a self made man who had risen from being a railway worker to become a leading electrical engineer. He studied to ever higher levels to become an AMIEE. At one stage he was the electrical consultant for the building of Sheffield University's Department of Applied Science in Mappin Street. He worked closely with the medical specialists of the day on the development of x-ray equipment.

Born in 1874 T W Sampson had his own manufacturing business during the first world war producing special switching devices. After the war the demand fell and most of his work was with Marsh Bros where he concentrated on electro-medical work. At first the new firm operated from Sampson's house in Sandford Grove Road, Netheredge.

Whilst Sampson's main line was electro-medical appliances there was not enough work for his electricians, this prompted him to take on general contracting work. That general work built up until by 1935 he had work at the Royal Infirmary, the Edgar

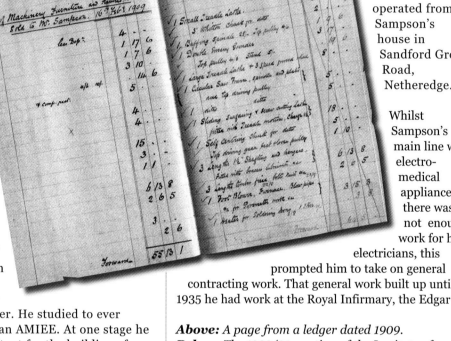

**Above:** *A page from a ledger dated 1909.*
**Below:** *The 1920/21 meeting of the Institute of Electrical Engineeres (South Yorkshire region).*

Allen Institute, Boots, Victoria Hall and many one off jobs. Sampson was also the agent for Newton Wright the x-ray manufacturer and for Associated Fire Alarms of Leicester. This last brought installation work and maintenance at two Carters factories, two of Bassets, Workshops for the Blind, the Sheffield Telegraph, Derbyshire Times and later Pickerings and Hadfields. The build up of business became too much for it to continue from Sampson's home where his clerical work was done by his daughter Dorothy and the move to Pitt Street was arranged.

Pitt Street then was a very different place than it is now. At the bottom was Portobello Steel Works complete with two converting furnaces. Opposite the Electron Works but fronting on to Mappin Street was a large building housing a number of small traders in the cutlery trade. One who had his door opposite made bone handles for knives: the raw bones arrived in very smelly loads which were dumped outside the door. The remainder of the street was lined with cottage property except for the blacksmith and the small public house. Today only the pub remains.

With the new premises new organisation was required. John Chadwick who had married Dorothy Sampson came to act as clerk. He had previously worked for T W Wards. Gordon Wilson was taken on as office boy. One Albert Oates was due to complete his apprenticeship shortly and a request was made to the Labour Exchange for an electrical apprentice. During the school holidays Stanley Hague had been attending the Labour exchange twice each week without success. On the last day before he was due to go back to school he called again and was given the card to see Mr Sampson; the following Monday he was signed up as an indentured apprentice to Mr Sampson.

The hourly rates of pay in the first year were 3d rising in the fifth and final year to 8d. The working week was 48 hours; a qualified journeyman electrician then got 1s 7d per hour.

**Above left:** *An early company letterhead.*
**Below:** *Mr John Chadwick (former managing director) on the left.*

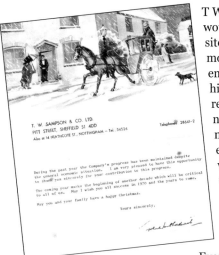

T W Sampson would visit each site every Friday morning paying employees from his purse and requesting a note of how many hours each had worked: this was often given on the back of a cigarette packet. Eventually more conventional procedures were adopted.

Work during the four years up to the start of the second world war increased and many large installations were carried out such as the University Union Building, Hallamshire Maternity Hospital, Ecclesfield Modern school, Conisbrough Convalescent home (later Conisbrough Council Office) and one floor of the Miners' block of the Royal Hospital. X-ray equipment was installed at the Devonshire Hospital, Buxton, Batley Hospital, Mexborough Montague Hospital and many others.

At that time most of the electrical installations in new buildings were in metal pipes; bending was done by means of wood setting-blocks not by bending machines. Holes for fixing were drilled by hammer and Rawlplug tools rather than today's power drills; in concrete this was slow and sure to raise blisters. Because Sheffield Corporation and the railways used wood capping and casing to cover cables apprentices were taught to how to use wood too, Sampsons used the half round 'Mackenite' wood capping which was difficult to work round corners. An interesting complication in those days was that different electricity tariffs meant separate meters for outside lighting, shop windows, indoor lighting, power and heating: in large shops the wiring could become a complicated mess.

T W Sampson died in 1938 aged 64. Ownership passed to his son-in-law John Chadwick and to former works foreman, Ted Oxley, a partnership which would last until Oxley's death in the 1960s.

By the end of the war the firm was employing around 24 staff and over the next twenty years continued to prosper.

In 1967 the firm opened branch offices in Nottingham. The following year it took over the long established

company of H G Freeman of Sidney Street, Sheffield, the directors at that time being J W Chadwick, G H Kay, H G Freeman, D Chadwick and J M Fisher.

John Chadwick died 1977 and ownership of the firm passed to G H Kay. Geoff Kay was a well known figure, a member of the National Board for the Electrical Contracting Industry and an Employer Member of the National Appeals Committee dealing with disputes. He began his working life with the company at the bottom of the ladder and eventually worked his way up to managing director.

J Michael Jackman, who joined the company in 1967, together with Paul Davis, another long serving member of the company, bought out Geoff Kay's interest in the firm in January 1989. The new partnership succeeded in doubling turnover in the following six years and continues its expansion plan. Today the business enters the third millennium with its reputation for service and quality as high as when T W Sampson founded the firm so many years ago.

***Above:*** *A letterhead from the 1960s.*
***Above right:*** *Mr Geoff Kay, former managing director.* ***Right:*** *From left to right: John Michael Jackman, Mrs S Oades, Paul Davis, Mr PJL Glover.*

# *Edwin Blyde - at the cutting edge for 200 years*

When Edwin Blyde began the business that still bears his name more than two centuries later, Admiral Nelson and the Duke of Wellington were still some years away from their finest hours. The French and the Americans had not long had their revolutions and the age of the industrial revolution had begun to take hold. In 1798, Edwin established a small cutlery and tools business. Little is known about those early days because few records were kept. The business was not registered at Company House until 1870.

In the years in between it looks as though Edwin was the 19th century equivalent of a wheeler dealer. He acquired a number of smaller companies that had particular special-

ities and retained the best skilled craftsmen from them. All the while he was expanding the business and developing the expertise it could offer.

***Above left:*** *Walter Trickett.* ***Above:*** *Stanley Trickett.* ***Below:*** *A staff photograph dated 1919.*

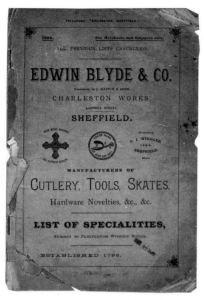

The earliest location of the company that can be traced is one in Lambert Street, from where it operated in the late 1800s.

In those days Edwin Blyde's offered a variety of products. There were table and pocket knives, cutlery, scissors, razors, saws, files and edging tools. The 1886 trade catalogue lists a gentleman's oak chest as being available for the princely sum of 5s 3d (26p). As well as the magnificent container, you also got a handsaw, mallet, pincers, hammer, bradawl, chisel, gouge, turnscrew and rule. Not bad for the price of a packet of chewing gum today. You could even get a pair of ice skates from Blyde's. Whizzing across frozen ponds was a popular Victorian pastime.

Around the beginning of the 20th century the business moved to Orange Street. In 1912, Walter Trickett purchased the company. Any association with the Blyde family ended there. It was the Tricketts who became the new dynasty of cutlers, though the business now focuses on pewter ware. Dennis Trickett, Walter's grandson, is the man at the helm today, keeping the family spirit of the company well and truly alive.

When Walter bought the company there had been a general move away from the tools and joinery links of the business. This seemed to him to be the right direction in which to take the company. He concentrated on building up the knife and cutlery side of the trade. He was experienced in the industry as a spoon and fork manufacturer and began to manufacture and sell a complete set of cutlery in its own container, known as the canteen of cutlery. Its popularity for wedding,

anniversary and celebratory presents made a successful reality of Walter Trickett's change of direction.

In the 1930s, each member of Bolton Wanderer's FA Cup team received a souvenir canteen to acknowledge their achievements. In 1912 Walter installed HC Gomm, a former Blyde employee, as company manager and continued to own and run both his companies side by side with one another. He was a strong and devout member of the Plymouth Brethren. Walter used to travel the country spreading his faith and looking for new converts. Unfortunately, his commitment to his beliefs was his undoing. One day in 1924, whilst preaching on the sands at Llandudno, he collapsed and died. As he was still only in his 50s, his death came as a shock to the family. Fortunately, son Walter Stanley Trickett had been sent to work at Blyde's in 1915, as a 14 year old. He had concentrated on learning about the hand crafting of the knife side of the business. Despite his youth, he took over the running of Blyde's and saw it through the usual ups and downs of any business, continuing to develop it as one of Sheffield's premier companies. He died in 1980. Trickett's original company was taken over after old Walter's death by Ronald Trickett, who had been with the company since 1920.

A major shift in emphasis came in the second half of the 20th century. Close to the premises on Orange Street was a small pewter business, James Furniss. It was decided to take over the company and incorporate some of the speciality of Furniss within the Blyde business. This was almost a throwback to the days when Edwin Blyde was collecting other companies and their skills around him. At the time the older types of companies were making cruets and tea sets out of pewter, silver plating them and shipping them off to Scotland and overseas. It was later that a pewter finish was seen to be sufficient in itself.

***Top:*** *An early brochure.* ***Above:*** *Early products by Edwin Blyde in the mid 20th century.*

The 1960s and 1970s were the days of the tankard. Leaving presents from work, 21st birthdays and prizes in competitions saw a forest of tankards appear on mantelpieces and bar room counters across the nation. The Furniss company was kept on as a separate company until the late 1970s, before it's work was fully incorporated into Blyde's business. The growth in the pewter trade saw the establishment of the Association of British Pewter Craftsmen in 1971.

Cutlery and knife production continued until the late 1980s, but cheap imports from abroad had reduced its importance to the company. It made Blyde's concentrate on its pewter trade. By 1980, Dennis Trickett had organised the purchase of the property at Little London Road. By 1989 he had met his current partners, Derek Stone and Jim and John Trower. They owned a pewter manufacturing business and it was natural that they joined forces. The expertise of the 'pewter men', allied with the reputation and experience of Blyde's, was a marriage made in heaven. Since then the company has grown stronger in both home and overseas markets. Now dealing solely in hand crafted pewter ware, Blyde's provides tankards, frames, flasks and trophies of quality.

**Above:** *Staff pictured in the 1960s.*
**Left:** *Products from the firm's current brochure.*

# The flower of Sheffield

Sheffield's oldest wholesale flower merchant, based in the Parkway wholesale market is the firm of Enos Kay Ltd.

The business was established in 1895 by the original Enos Kaye, a Sheffield man who began his fledgling firm of fruit and flower merchants in the Castlefields wholesale market, sited where the Park Square roundabout is today.

In those far off days there were of course very few imported fruit and flowers, how times have changed!

Cecil Kaye followed his father Enos into the business at the end of the first world war and ran it until the 1960s when Castlefields market closed. Allan Kirk then took over the company he had joined in 1926 and ran it until his death in March 1976.

Allan Kirk had at first worked as a porter before working his way into sales, whilst Cecil Kaye ran the office.

The bulk of the business was built up during the 1950s and 60s when the trade in British cut flowers was in its height. After the austerity of the war years, entertaining at home and home decor with flowers was high on people's agenda.

In the 1960s Allan bought stock from the prominent growing areas of Lincolnshire and around Blackpool. By then Kaye's was handling 2,000 heavy wooden boxes of blooms each day. Not everyone was happy however: Mrs Kirk was always annoyed at Allan because, typical of his generation, he always wore collar tie and suit to market and every one of his suits quickly acquired a telltale dark stain on the shoulder from carrying boxes of flowers and plants.

Nursery owners who had come back from the Great War however had by the 1960s got to the end of their working lives; many nurseries closed because the market was difficult and land held more value for development. Allan Kirk and his colleagues went so far as to acquire their own nursery in Wisbech but it was short-lived. When Allan was chatting to fellow customers in a pub one evening they told him they had been in Norfolk and pulled into a nursery where the manager let them take as much as they wanted for nothing - it turned out to be Allan's Nursery and his manager!

Adrian Kirk joined his father Allan in 1973 on leaving school. One of Adrian's earliest childhood recollections is seeing 4,000 Christmas trees being delivered and having to be transported to the shops around Sheffield because there was nowhere to store them.

Sadly Allan Kirk's health failed and he was unable to show Adrian the ropes as he would have wished. The business soon experienced difficulties: the 'Winter of Discontent' saw Enos Kaye staff on a three day week. Other businesses failed but Kaye's survived, picking up customers from those who fell by the wayside.

*Above: Even the war has its happy side.*
***Right:** Adrian takes an early shine to gardening.*

A decade later the business had turned the corner and was growing. Many changes had occurred: the seasonality of the flower trade lost its effect when products such as chrysanthemums and lilies from Holland, spray carnations from Israel and Colombian carnations could be easily and quickly imported.

Once the firm had to order flowers a week in advance: today a phone call by 10 am on one day sees blooms on sale by 4 am the next. Temperature controlled transport ensures that stock now arrives from all corners of the world in perfect condition.

Demand for flowers and plants has soared over the last ten years as television programmes have helped make gardening an increasingly popular pastime.

Enos Kaye is today Sheffield's foremost wholesaler providing customer service second to none with more than century of learning and experience

behind it. The firm covers an area taking in Doncaster, Gainsborough, Matlock, Penistone, Barnsley and Scunthorpe.

The variety of products offered from quality growers increases on a daily basis with a new bloom or plant being offered almost every 24 hours. Fruit and vegetables are still sold alongside flowers whilst since the gardening boom Kaye's also carries compost, green bags and other gardening sundries.

A third generation of the Kirk family will soon come into the business as Adrian's son Adam is eager to leave school and join his father, promising a blooming 21st century for this Sheffield firm with its roots in the 19th.

***Above:*** *The early involvement with the Crysanthemum Society.* ***Below:*** *A staff gathering outside the firm's premises in the 1980s.*

# Success in every department

Can there be anyone in Sheffield who, over the years, has not visited Atkinsons department store? Back in 1997 Atkinsons celebrated 125 years of service to the Sheffield public.

Like many thriving business Atkinsons had humble origins. The firm was founded by John Atkinson who arrived in Sheffield in 1865 to seek his fortune. After working as a sales representative at the age of 26, in 1872, and with very little capital, John Atkinson launched his business from 90 South Street, Sheffield Moor dealing in lace, ribbons, and hosiery. From the outset he provided helpful service, good quality merchandise and value for money - the three ingredients of successful retailing.

By 1879 John Atkinson was so successful that his small shop was bursting at the seams and he took over two neighbouring shops, numbers 88 and 86.

At first number 86 was let out but five years later it was brought into the fold and equipped as a millinery department.

In 1887 three shops were acquired in Prince Street and opened as furniture showrooms, a new venture which John Atkinson plunged into with his customary business flair and drive.

Harold and Walter Atkinson soon joined the firm with the same dedication and enthusiasm as their father. A showroom for the shawl and mantle trade was opened behind Prince Street. Though growing in importance and prospering the business was however still basically six shops knocked into one and John Atkinson began to dream of the day when he would own his own department store.

The year of the big leap forward was 1892 when shops and land at 76-86 South Street were bought; five years later space at the back of 86 and 88 was bought and a new dress warehouse opened.

1901 saw the foundation stone laid of an all-in-one store which was completed the following year.

**Above:** *An early advertisement.*
**Below:** *The Millinery showroom in 1910.*
**Bottom:** *The store in 1902.*

This gave the Atkinsons an extra floor; so many customers flocked to the store that a small army of assistants was need to cope. John Atkinson's dream had been realised.

During the first world war Atkinsons continued to grow even though part of the premises were requisitioned as machine shops to produce war supplies. By 1918 further extensions were needed; ready to wear fashions were now playing a large part whilst the store had branched out to specialise in furs.

By the firm's golden jubilee in 1922, seven years before the founder's death, the store housed 46 departments.

The most dramatic year in the history of Atkinsons however was 1940. In December of that year the Germans launched their Blitz on Sheffield and in one night everything that the Atkinson family had built up over the

*Above:* Atkinson's was razed to the ground in the blitz of 1940. **Top:** Atkinson's decorated for a celebration in 1905.

previous 68 years was destroyed. Employees turning up for work the next day found nothing but rubble. Money left in the store had melted into a single mass.

Harold and Walter Atkinson now showed their flair for improvisation; within just a few weeks they opened for business again in temporary premises in St Judes Church and schoolroom in Milton street. The various departments were dispersed to premises at Johnson and Appleyard in Leopold Street, James Lamb on the Moor and even the Central Cinema. It was to be twenty years before the store could come together under one roof again.

Immediately after the war Atkinsons bought Tuckwoods high class grocers in Fargate which was turned into a department store and food hall with restaurant. In 1947 J.Walter Atkinson died; his brother Harold survived him by another eleven years, celebrating his fiftieth anniversary with the firm in 1954.

Atkinsons present department store in the Moor finally opened in 1960.

In 1975 the chairman, Walter Atkinson's son Peter, invited Sainsbury's to set up shop alongside his own; that £1,500,000 plan benefited both companies not least by providing a multi-storey car park.

The year 2000 saw the Atkinsons store expand by 50 per cent at the first floor level: the furniture area has been doubled, more fashion concessions were introduced along with an electrical department and a third restaurant.

Today the fourth generation of the family has the confidence and expertise to ensure that what John Atkinson founded in the 19th century is geared up to meet the challenges of the 21st.

# The (sur)face work of precision engineering

**A**lbert Marsh and Bestelite is better known in the world of surface engineering as AMB. This snappier title reflects the form of precision engineering that the company undertakes. The company was formed with the merger of two well established companies, Albert Marsh and Co and Bestelite (Hardfacing) Ltd. The company has developed into the nation's leader in hardsurfacing in the pump and valve industry. No part, from regulators on steam valves, is too small nor any too large, such as massive sea water injection pumps in the oil industry, for AMB. It supplies many of the country's hot steel rolling mills with guide rollers that are deposited with Stellite. This is a remarkable hardfacing alloy that, although relatively expensive, can be applied to a roller of cheaper metal. This cobalt based alloy dramatically reduces roller wear and proves cost effective in the long run.

The original company was set up by Albert Marsh in 1938. He was a skilled engineer with wide experience of his trade gained from work in a number of Sheffield industries. His colleagues were taken aback when this fine craftsman decided to chance his arm as a businessman, but he was soon to make his mark. He established his first premises on Portobello Street. Brick linings for refractors were the mainstay of the business. In the beginning, custom was drawn from local businesses and Albert's venture was just a small enterprise that seemed to be slow in taking off.

But the world was to be turned upside down as the jackboots of history tramped across Belgium and Poland. Albert's little business was suddenly turned into a major war effort. The government needed armaments to fight the second world war and the brick lining business was transformed overnight into a 24 hour production line. Over 50 people, almost exclusively female, were employed to serve the war effort. But the works on Portobello Street did not survive the bombs of the Luftwaffe. A direct hit on the factory was also a blow against Britain. However, from the ruins of the first premises, the business quickly transferred to a new site on Solly

**Above:** *Albert Marsh.*
**Right:** *Mr Newbould.*

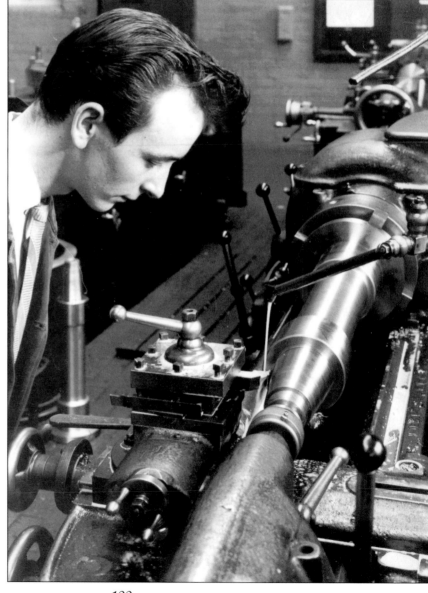

Street and production was restarted in earnest. Before the end of the war Albert's wife became a director, though she played no day to day role until after the war.

When the dust settled after the armistice was signed, Albert Marsh's company returned to its traditional refractory work. It continued in much the same vein for the next decade, but the seeds of change were sown in 1954 when Albert's daughter married Mr Hall, today's company chairman. Mr Hall had trained as an accountant and brought his business skills to bear when he was brought into the company fold in September 1960. By this time, Albert Marsh was in poor health. Sadly, he was not to recover his strength and died two years later. Bert Butterworth, then a foreman, took over the day to day running during Mr Marsh's illness.

*Above: The company's premises today. **Top:** Modern machinery capable of manufacturing high quality finished components to customers' designs. **Right:** Mr BC Hall.*

However, the financial side of the business was in need of an overhaul and Mr Hall recognised that his accountancy experience was to be the company's saviour. If he had not stepped in, Marsh's would have had to have been sold. Bert was given the task of supervising the works whilst Mr Hall handled the management and financial side of things. His was the guiding hand that took the company from the brink of closure to the success it has become today. He had a number of contacts in the engineering industry. Soon after taking charge he joined forces with a friend, Jim Bardsley. He was the head salesman for Stellite. It was through this relationship that the company that was to become AMB began manufacturing Stellite rollers. Scunthorpe Rod Mill was the first customer, but the business soon went from strength to strength to reach its current position as the country's top name in production. By the time of Mr Hall's retirement in the early 1990s, AMB had grown out of all proportion to the little business that Albert Marsh had begun. The present MD, Mr Newbould, who joined straight from the army in 1964, is also looking further ahead as the company develops its website to attract even wider business.

# *Sawing a slice of history*

The well-known Sheffield firm of Wolstenholme Machine Knives Ltd was founded in 1908, though not incorporated until 1946. The founder was Thomas Gilbert Wolstenholme, a big man in every sense of the word and one who physically towered over most of his contemporaries.

T G Wolstenholme originally worked for W A Tyzack, a famous local company, as a saw maker or 'smither'. The young man decided he wanted to set up on his own account making new saws and resetting old ones. Going to see Mr Tyzack and informing him of his intentions Mr Tyzack demanded time to think about it. A week later Tyzack approached Thomas Wolstenholme and offered to take all the saws he could produce rather than be competitors for the same business. So T G Wolstenholme set up on his own and Mr Tyzack filled his factory, the embryonic Wolstenholme company becoming exclusive suppliers to Tyzack - a business relationship which would persist to the early 1930s.

Both companies benefited from the arrangement - Tyzacks getting a cheap local supplier and T G Wolstenholme his own business.

The Great War took Thomas Wolstenholme away from Sheffield to do his bit for king and country; on his return in 1918 he used his gratuity to purchase his first major piece of equipment - a lathe which today has pride of place in the reception area at the firm's Clough Bank Works.

The original business concentrated on circular saws. Much of the production of huge six foot diameter saws went to logging concerns in Canada and North America although it was not until 1964 that the firm's achieved its first major export order to the USA, a country which now provides the company's single largest market.

The firm's first premises were in Sheffield's Edmund Road, a four storey building which originally housed two companies and which over the years was extended eventually taking the whole site incorporating a barrel yard; later houses were purchased along the road.

By 1994 the company used about 10,000 square feet and could expand no further on the site even though had moved some production to Roman Ridge Road.

***Above:*** *Thomas Gilbert Wolstenholme, founder.*
***Below:*** *One of the company's earliest products.*

The Roman Ridge Road site had in fact been bought in 1987 to take care of circular saw production whilst Edmund Road concentrated on straight blades. The Roman Ridge Road premises however proved to be only a temporary move and in 1996 the firm moved again to the present premises purpose built premises the Clough Works Downgate Drive.

Today, as in the past, more than three quarters of production goes in exports. The connections established with North America so may years ago are stronger than ever with a subsidiary in America TGW Inc formed in 1994 based in Cincinnati and a sub office in Chicago and New England with plans to expand into Texas and the West Coast to provide comprehensive cover for the whole North American market. The firm is now moving strongly into Europe and is moving forward into Japan and the far East.

The company remains privately owned with the present managing director Richard Wolstenholme the great grandson of the founder Thomas Wolstenholme and

*Top: Alf Wolstenholme (left), second generation.*
*Above: Tom (left) and Fred Wolstenholme who represent the third generation.* **Right:** *The company's premises today.*

whose father Fred and grandfather Alf had preceded him in the company.

Up until the third generation the Wolstenholme family were able to remain hands-on owners even though by 1950 they employed some 30 staff. Today the group employs approximately 100 people.

Today the firm uses computers and lasers which have largely taken over from hand tools and hand grinding skills. In place of saws, the firm now produces cutting blades for use by the packaging, food processing and paper industries. Not even the present managing director's father would recognise the firm today with over two million pounds recently invested in state of the art equipment in a little over two years - £200,000 on IT alone.

In a highly specialised market the firm is, like its founder, a giant amongst its competitors, but in real terms still small enough to sell a commodity based on the experience of decades and one which can supply small batches of its products. And if the founder might have difficulty recognising today's firm he would at least recognise the principles which underpin it and take pride in the knowledge that his name today is synonymous with an excellent saw tooth.

# *Keeping even Houdini safe*

The days are long gone when you could leave your door unlocked when you popped down the road to the corner shop. Nowadays, not only has the corner shop disappeared, but, by the time you got back, so would your TV, video and stereo system. We have had to become more security conscious. Ordinary homes now have window locks, five lever mortice door locks, burglar alarms, security lights and panic buttons. It is a sad reflection on the times in which we live.

Our schools have been turned into fortresses with exit only doors and intercom systems to connect with the secretary's office. There are CCTV cameras in offices, car parks, shopping centres and on the High Street. Our valuables are in safes and our cars are protected with immobilisers. It is a different world from the one William Harrold knew when he began his locksmith, whitesmith and bell hanging business, however, locksmithing soon took over as a full time occupation.

It was in 1919, just after the first world war, when he moved from Derby to open his premises on Burgess Street, a site much later to be taken over by Cole Bros. These days the company operates out of Shalesmoor, Sheffield S3 from one of the largest Locksmithing Companies in the UK, including its very own conference suite. Still very much a family company today, dealing with all aspects of the security business, it employs 19 staff. A back up fleet of well-equipped vans can see H Harrold and Sons Ltd responding to call outs from much further afield than just the Sheffield area, however in the beginning it was a modest venture. All the work was done by hand. Some of that old craftsmanship was passed on through successive generations. Even in the 1950s locksmiths had to cut intricate keys by hand.

In the 1940s and early 1950s there were no company vehicles, locksmiths had to carry their toolbags and equipment and travel by tram and bus. There were very few locksmiths capable of opening safes at this time and work was carried out for many titled families at their historic homes in Yorkshire and Derbyshire. Travelling to jobs further afield meant catching a train at the old Victoria Station and sometimes took all day. The first vehicle was a 1938 Wolsey 12 purchased in 1949 followed by the Company's first van a Morris Minor which was obtained in 1958. However, it was a much earlier event that was to help change the fortunes of the company and make the name of William Harrold known to a much wider audience.

Harry Houdini was in town. The famous escapologist of the early 20th century was one of the top entertainers of his day. Crowds flocked to see his act. He would get out of the most amazing series of locks, padlocks and chains, much to the astonishment of the watching multitudes.

***Above:*** *An 18th century Box or Wards Key.* ***Below:*** *H Harrold & Sons' first premises at Rockingham Lane.*

Sometimes he would be suspended from a crane, sometimes he would be underwater. How did he do it? William Harrold could have told them. His reputation as a locksmith had reached Houdini's ears. The great showman commissioned William to make some stage props that he used in his act however, true to his profession, William Harrold kept the tricks of the trade as secure as one of his own padlocks. Houdini's secrets were safe with him.

In 1938 a fire destroyed the Albert Hall and the surrounding premises, including William Harrold's workshop, which were condemned for demolition. William Harrold moved first to Rockingham Lane and then to Division Street when security became a retail business. Security became especially important during the war years. The company was very busy doing work for the armed forces and the steel industry. Air raids caused widespread damage. Many a time safes had to be located in bombed out premises and opened where they stood in dangerous surroundings. After the war, William's son, Henry, took over the company. Henry as a young man was a very good footballer and was on the books of Sheffield Wednesday, however he was under 21 and his father refused to allow him to sign professional

forms. In the early 1900s football was not considered a suitable profession and so he entered locksmithing. He later married Iva Alice Kenyon the daughter of Reece Kenyon a Loxley mill owner. The Kenyons were a well known Loxley family going back many generations. Of great historical interest is their original mill up the Loxley valley at Little Matlock. Little Matlock rolling mill is one of the few remaining water powered mills still in existance. It is at present under a preservation order and hopefully will be preserved for future generations. When they involved their sons, Terry, Norman and Gordon, they soon built it up into a thriving and well respected business. Terry was one of the last articled locksmiths in the trade. In the 1970s the firm was expanded by the addition of another six family members. They included the current management team of Tony, Peter and Diane.

The company has remained successful by keeping up with the great technological strides the business world has made over the last decade. H Harrold & Sons Ltd is a leader in the development of CCTV systems and digital, card and phone entry systems. However, it still maintains traditional lines. There are extensive showrooms where over 250 safes are kept in stock, all with a comprehensive after sales service. The company have fully trained safe engineers who with today's technology and equipment originally designed for the medical profession can offer a non-destructive safe opening service. These flexi-scopes using fibre optics costing many thousands of pounds are used to identify problems in the most intricate safe locks and mechanisms. Just to show that some things never change, the company was recently asked to advise an escapologist on developing his act!

**Top:** *The premises on Division Street.*
**Above:** *An advertisement which appeared in the Sheffield Telegraph in 1958.* **Right:** *The current premises.*

A picture of the busy Haymarket, seen here on a rainy day in 1946

# *Acknowledgments*

*The publishers would like to thank Sheffield City Council and Sheffield Central Library -*
*in particular Mr D Hindmarch and Mr Mike Spick of the Local Studies Department.*
*South Yorkshire Police Press and Public Relations Department.*

*Thanks are also due to*
*Peggy Burns who penned the editorial text*
*and Steve Ainsworth for his copywriting skills*